NO MORE PHONICS AND SPELLING WORKSHEETS

Dear Readers,

Much like the diet phenomenon *Eat This, Not That*, this series aims to replace some existing practices with approaches that are more effective—healthier, if you will—for our students. We hope to draw attention to practices that have little support in research or professional wisdom and offer alternatives that have greater support. Each text is collaboratively written by authors representing research and practice. Section 1 offers a practitioner's perspective on a practice in need of replacing and helps us understand the challenges, temptations, and misunderstandings that have led us to this ineffective approach. Section 2 provides a researcher's perspective on the lack of research to support the ineffective practice(s) and reviews research supporting better approaches. In Section 3, the author representing a practitioner's perspective gives detailed descriptions of how to implement these better practices. By the end of each book, you will understand both what not to do, and what to do, to improve student learning.

It takes courage to question one's own practice—to shift away from what you may have seen throughout your years in education and toward something new that you may have seen few if any colleagues use. We applaud you for demonstrating that courage and wish you the very best in your journey from this to that.

Best wishes,
—*Nell K. Duke and Ellin Oliver Keene, series editors*

No More Phonics and Spelling Worksheets

JENNIFER L. PALMER

MARCIA INVERNIZZI

HEINEMANN
Portsmouth, NH

Heinemann
361 Hanover Street
Portsmouth, NH 03801–3912
www.heinemann.com

Offices and agents throughout the world

The authors and publisher wish to thank those who have generously given permission to reprint borrowed material:

Figure 2–3: From *Words Their Way: Word Study for Phonics, Vocabulary, and Spelling Instruction*, 5th edition, by Donald R. Bear, Marcia A. Invernizzi, Shane R. Templeton, and Francine R. Johnson. Copyright © 2012. Printed and electronically adapted by permission of Pearson Education, Inc., Upper Saddle River, New Jersey.

Figure 2–4: From "Developmental-Spelling Research: A Systematic Imperative" by Marcia Invernizzi and Latisha Hayes in *Reading Research Quarterly*, Volume 39, Issue 2 (2004). Copyright © 2004 by International Reading Association. Article first published online November 9, 2011. Reprinted by permission of John Wiley and Sons conveyed through Copyright Clearance Center.

Library of Congress Cataloging-in-Publication Data
Palmer, Jennifer L.
   No more phonics and spelling worksheets / Jennifer Palmer and
Marcia Invernizzi.
         pages cm – (Not this, but that)
   Includes bibliographical references.
   ISBN 978-0-325-04797-3
   1. Reading—Phonetic method. 2. English language—Orthography and
spelling—Study and teaching. 3. Language arts.   I. Invernizzi, Marcia.   II. Title.

LB1573.3.P45 2014
372.46'5—dc23   2014021492

Series editors: Nell K. Duke *and* Ellin Oliver Keene
Editor: Margaret LaRaia
Production: Vicki Kasabian
Interior design: Suzanne Heiser
Cover design: Lisa A. Fowler
Typesetter: Valerie Levy, Drawing Board Studios
Manufacturing: Veronica Bennett

Printed in the United States of America on acid-free paper
18   VP   4   5

CONTENTS

Section 3   BUT THAT

53 **Deep Engagement With Words**
Jennifer Palmer

INTRODUCTION

NELL K. DUKE

Explicitly teaching sound–letter relationships and their application to reading and writing improves reading and writing achievement. There is perhaps no educational-research finding better supported than this. And yet there is perhaps no area of instruction that is more variously— and more poorly—taught. I have seen teachers teaching phonics "rules" that studies show apply far less than half the time. I have seen children given endless stacks of worksheets that they could only complete if they already knew the material. In classroom after classroom I have seen all children being given the same spelling lists despite considerable research demonstrating that that is less effective than a differentiated approach. Most importantly, I have seen a topic that is potentially engaging for children reduced to rote drudgery.

Given all this, Ellin and I were very eager to elicit a book for this series on doing phonics and spelling instruction better—in a way that reflects the extensive research in this area and the wisdom of professional practice. And we were very eager to get Jennifer Palmer and Marcia Invernizzi on board—the perfect pair to do this book. Jennifer's extensive experience in low socioeconomic schools and her commitment to creating research-based learning experiences for children made her the natural choice for this book. Marcia Invernizzi is a world-renowned scholar, whose career has been marked by the ability to not only conduct first-rate research but also to bring research-based practice to practitioners throughout the United States and beyond.

Ellin and I could not be more pleased to bring this book to you. We hope you too will be pleased by the opportunity to make your phonics and spelling instruction as effective and engaging as it can be.

SECTION 1
NOT THIS

Worksheets/Workbooks: The Trap of Repetition Without Transfer

JENNIFER PALMER

Most of us who go into education love children. I'm pretty typical. I wanted to work with children and make a difference in their lives. I went to college. I took classes on how to teach. I learned theory. I student-taught. I loved school and watched many teachers at work during my own schooling. I constructed an image of what teachers should do. I thought I knew what a classroom should look like and what learning was, but I based this image on my own experiences. I went into my classroom, closed my door, and taught the way I had been taught when I went to school. It took a long time before I examined my own vision of what teachers should do when they teach spelling or phonics. I simply reenacted what I believed teachers were supposed to do, until I realized that there was a disconnect between how students learn to read and spell and the way I was teaching.

Before I began teaching first grade, I was a long-term substitute in a third-grade classroom. I used the spelling lists in the basal reader teacher's manual, but they seemed to have no connection to the stories or to the related phonics lessons. After a few frustrating weeks, I asked other teachers in my building what they used.

I found they had abandoned the basal lists; each teacher developed a spelling list based on the social studies or science units they were currently teaching. This made a lot of sense: It reinforced the words students were learning in the content areas, helped them make cross-curricular connections, and encouraged them to use the words in other contexts. The parents I talked to supported my efforts to align spelling with content and were pleased that I was keeping expectations high.

For my first list, I used words from our weather unit: *cumulus, stratus, cirrus, barometer*, and sixteen more. Students took the pretest and identified the words they needed to study. Their homework followed this weekly pattern:

- On Monday night, they looked up the words in a dictionary (students shouldn't have to spell words whose meaning they don't know).
- On Tuesday night they put the words in alphabetical order.
- On Wednesday night they searched for examples of the words in print.
- On Thursday night they wrote each word five times on a study sheet and then had a parent quiz them.

Come Friday morning, the students numbered their papers from 1 through 20 and dutifully wrote down the words as I dictated: "*Cumulus. Cumulus is a fair-weather cloud. Cumulus.*" I collected the papers and graded them. The scores fell into a typical bell curve, and I was satisfied. At first.

However, as the weeks passed, I noticed that many students who spelled the words correctly on the Friday tests misspelled them in their science papers and journals. *Barometer* was spelled BARAHMITR. *Cirrus* was spelled SIROUS or CIRUS or even SEERUS. Words that had been so industriously learned were quickly forgotten. It was frustrating for me and for the kids. I presented review lessons. I asked parents to review words from previous lessons. We had spelling bees. We created mnemonics ("there is *a rat* in sep-*a rat*-e"). Nothing seemed to help. I had to explain to parents that students who had aced every spelling test were getting Cs in spelling on their report cards because they were misspelling the words in their written work. Their word knowledge wasn't transferring, and I was holding them (not me) responsible.

The Factory Model of Teaching Ignores Transference

Lack of transference wasn't isolated to spelling tests but in other areas of literacy instruction as well. The third-grade phonics curriculum included more complex combinations of letters and sounds. These "pals" were supposed to help students decode multisyllable words. I would teach the kids words containing a particular combination, and they would fill in a worksheet. For example: I showed them *-ation*; we read a list of words containing *-ation* (*nation, elation, frustration, situation*); and they then created sentences using these words. I graded these worksheets at night, satisfied that students had learned the sound the letter combination represented. But, again, many kids weren't able to apply what they had learned when they came across a word with *-ation* in it the very next day.

How do you get students to remember words? You'll learn the principles behind this kind of instruction in Section 2 and be given specific practices to use in your own classroom in Section 3

Looking back, I see one source of my difficulties. I was following the "factory model" of spelling and decoding, in which students were the recipients of the "knowledge" I was dumping into their heads:

- I made no attempt to help students link their spelling words with their current understanding of how words work.

- I didn't show students how knowing *-ation* would help them figure out a new word, nor did I help them see how knowing this pattern would help them spell.
- I didn't show students how to generalize what they had learned about spelling and apply it to new words.
- I didn't provide authentic opportunities to apply or practice phonics or word knowledge in real reading and writing.

No one can memorize the spelling of every single word in the English language, yet I taught both decoding and spelling as if this were the one true way to learn to read words and spell. Games like Concentration do not help students learn how to spell a word; activities like copying the word five times or writing the word in a sentence are not much better. Students learn that one word, letter by letter, and then forget it later. Flash cards are not much better either. Students may recognize the word on the card but not when it appears in text.

What are some other myths about English spelling that misinform our instruction?

see Section 2, page 28

My students saw spelling as something they did on a test, not something they applied to their reading and writing; they saw phonics as separate from real reading and spelling. Without a reason to learn, students were motivated only to reproduce the most superficial layer of behavior expected of them. They were factory workers contributing one small widget to a car whose make and model they didn't know or care about. Many of them were not transferring their ability to spell to their real writing, because I didn't expect them to. Many students were not using their knowledge of phonics to decode words when they were reading either, because I hadn't shown them how.

Many spelling and phonics activities do not allow for discussion, but I have found that the most effective practices require not only time for students to think but also time to talk with others about what we are learning. Why is a particular word spelled with an *ai* and not an *ay*? Why are *rain, plain, Spain,* and *again* spelled similarly but *again* doesn't have a long-*a* sound like the others (unless you're British). If kids notice that *ai* in the words *said, again,* and *against* sounds different than *ai* in *raid, gain,* and *explain,* questions naturally follow. If these words are spelled the same, why do they sound different?

When we engage students in discussion about these kinds of questions, we create curiosity and a desire to learn more about how words work. There is a particular study that Marcia references in the next section that demonstrates for us the power of student discussion in helping students to apply their learning to new reading and writing situations (Post and Carreker 2002). Yet we generally don't give kids time to think or to question or talk with one another about their thinking about words. Instead, we tell kids a particular rule and all the words that fit the rule. On Friday's test, they don't have to think about it. We don't give them the opportunity to make sense of English spelling.

Stopping the Assembly Line: Taking the Time to Think

My first principal encouraged teachers to think. She bought us journals and gave us time during faculty meetings to write about what in our teaching worked or didn't work. At first, writing about my decoding and spelling lessons was depressing. I wondered for a while whether journaling was good for my mental health. I kept uncovering more questions; I wasn't finding a lot of answers and when I talked to my colleagues I found that they had the same questions I had!

Eventually I realized that the questions that bubbled up repeatedly in my journal were important to my growth as a professional—that those questions were far more important than any immediate answers might be. The quiet time I carved out during my busy day to write about my struggles helped me become a more thoughtful teacher. Journaling, professional reading, and talking with colleagues about teaching are still a big part of my professional development as I continue to learn and grow.

I realized that I had a choice. I could continue to do what I had always done with spelling and decoding instruction—no one would criticize me if the students were still struggling as these students were considered challenging—or take a harder look at my own practices and try to find another way to meet my students' needs. For me, the choice was easy. I needed to reject the traditional methods of teaching spelling and decoding, which weren't working, in favor of facilitating more effective word study.

We need to be as engaged in and plugged into our work as we expect our students to be with theirs. We must become our own researchers, fearlessly examining our students' reaction to what we have taught. We need to be honest and open our classroom doors to colleagues who share our struggles and exchange ideas, learning and growing together. And we should encourage our colleagues to be part of this research community. I too have been beaten over the head with the term "research-based" and seen the damage caused when we try to apply research without truly understanding its meaning. I understand the negative, visceral reaction many of us have when we think of educational research, but it doesn't have to be that way. Here's what I started to notice when I began to reflect, ask questions, investigate current research, and experiment.

How Are Students Showing Their Learning: Engagement or Entertainment?

One year early in my teaching career, I gained ten pounds before Christmas because I ran for the nearest source of chocolate as soon as the buses left at the end of each day. That year almost every curriculum I taught was new or revised, district pressure to improve test scores was at fever pitch, and I had a class that was resistant to playing school. Nevertheless, I remember those twenty-four first graders with great affection, because they taught me so much. They were loving, creative, rambunctious, thoughtful, emotional, and full of potential, but it was tough to keep their attention.

In one unfortunate attempt to engage this group of students, I dressed up as an old grandmother to teach the "Digraph brothers"—Charles (*ch*), Thad (*th*), Whit (*wh*), and Shawn (*sh*). Some students got the giggles, some were obviously bored, and others kept getting the digraph sounds confused. I stopped mid-lesson; continuing was pointless. While the laughter showed I was entertaining some of my students—although, were they laughing *with* or *at* me?—I couldn't prove that they were learning.

Sometimes we identify the problem of students' lack of engagement and think that putting smiles on their faces can shift the learning. It's not that simple. There's a difference between true academic engagement and entertainment. Spelling bees, games, and fun phonics activities fail to motivate students to hold onto their learning (or to learn in the first place) because they're experiences decontextualized from real reading and writing. How do we get kids engaged in word learning? Marcia and I will answer these questions in Sections 2 and 3, but first let's address something that the lack of engagement tells us. Something we know as teachers but struggle to respond to.

One Size Doesn't Fit All

The factory model confuses compliance with learning. A student who completes his phonics or spelling worksheet every night is following directions, but not necessarily doing deep-level thinking or demonstrating independence. Furthermore, when we give every student the same worksheet, we communicate the unfair expectations that they all can and should learn the same words at the same time. Some students don't bother doing the worksheet because they've had too many experiences where they can't, and, in that scenario, the most logical behavior is to avoid further humiliation by turning *can't* into *won't*. Other students wonder why they have to do a worksheet when they already knew all the words on the Monday spelling pretest! The whole-class approach may reach some students, but it almost certainly wastes the time of most students. So, at its best, it's inefficient. We know students develop at different rates, so why would we think all kids are ready to learn the same phonics and spelling skills at the same time?

Malina was a member of the career-changing class of first graders I mentioned earlier. She was tall for her age, with beautiful eyes that at times sparkled with a natural curiosity and at other times were filled with self-doubt. She had a flair for drama and already at age six had learned how to get herself noticed.

Malina was taking a lot longer to learn to read and spell than the rest of the class, but she was just as motivated, at least at first. She loved stories; when I read picture books to the class at the end of each school day, she was mesmerized. She headed for the bus, her head swimming with characters and events from the story, often acting out her favorite part.

She came to first grade knowing the names and forms of the letters in her name but none of the sounds. She spent all her free time leafing through the picture books in our classroom library. She told me she wanted to be a writer and a movie star. She struggled with the phonics worksheets I gave the class as a way to learn letters. She glued the pictures that started with *b* under the letter *p*. She colored the pictures that ended with the target letter rather than the pictures that started with that letter. She sometimes refused to write unless I wrote first and she copied. Her mother had her practice recognizing words by sight using the flash cards I provided, but the words were gone by the time she got to school the next morning. She could neither read nor write them.

Malina's classroom behavior began to change every time we did something related to literacy. Right before a phonics lesson, she needed to go to the bathroom. Right before writing, her tummy started to hurt. During writing, she told me a fabulous story with fairy-tale princesses and dramatic rescues. But her story journal contained just the two words she knew, *I like*, and then a string of random letters: *ILIKEMDNWxGDY3st!* or *I LIKEDNMWsxt3YdG?* Every day she mixed up the letters she knew in a different order. Why were the phonics lessons I was teaching not taking? I presented word lists containing a particular digraph and we practiced reading them. Most of Malina's classmates were doing fine, learning to read and filling their journals with pages and pages of writing. What was the problem for Malina? Why couldn't she learn?

A conversation I had with the mother of one of Malina's classmates provided a glimmer of an answer. Cousins Alix and Becky were both in my class, and Alix's mom was a wonderfully supportive weekly volunteer. One day, she told me that Alix and Becky had been playing school since they were very little. They would take turns being the teacher and read to each other. It hit me. They were *already* readers and writers when they arrived in my classroom. They could do those phonics worksheets because they already *knew* the letters and their sounds.

Who else knew the sounds and letters featured in my basal lessons before I even taught them? I did a little pretest before the next lesson and discovered something that changed my teaching forever. The *vast majority* of the students who were successful on the phonics worksheets were those who already knew the sounds the letters represented.

I had been following the recommended process of presenting a letter and its accompanying sound to the class, asking the class chorally to read lists of words that contained that letter–sound, having one group read a basal story centered on that letter–sound while another group practiced it on worksheets, and then switching

How can we figure out what students know and need to know?

see Section 2, page 17

the groups. The students who knew the letter–sound already were able to complete the worksheet. The students who didn't, weren't. Not only were the worksheets a waste of time, so was the way I was presenting my phonics lessons. I was giving everyone the same lesson at the same time, whether or not it was the most appropriate next step for the student.

It was no different with my spelling lists. There were some students, like Juan, who already knew the list on the pretest and were already spelling the word correctly in everyday writing. There were others like Maria who learned the list for the test but failed to apply them in writing. And there were other students, like Jaden, who could never seem to master the words on the list, even if I reduced the number of words presented to them.

By paying attention to my students, I learned that the practices in place in my classroom were not effective. The question was not *What is wrong with Malina and Jaden?* It was *How do I move each of my students forward in their decoding and spelling skills?* There was something wrong with the strategies I was using to develop decoding and spelling skills in my students. I was not helping Malina or Jaden, who were emergent readers and writers. I was also doing a disservice to my early readers like Becky, Alix, and Maria—and to every other student in my class. Who really learns anything with the one-size-fits-all model?

It can seem overwhelming to consider true differentiated instruction, but in Sections 2 and 3 you'll see how manageable it can be—and more effective.

What Does Each Child Know and How Can I Teach from There?

We can cast off the one-size-fits-all factory instruction and pick up a more useful practice—meeting each child where she or he is. Spelling pretests tell us what words on the list kids know, but they don't help us decide what words or phonics patterns are appropriate for them to learn next. Through diagnostic assessment, we can determine what spelling and phonics knowledge students have and what they are ready to learn. You'll learn why starting with diagnostic assessment works and where to go from there in Sections 2 and 3.

There *Is* a Better Way

Don't we, as teachers, want our students to be excited and engaged in their learning? Don't we want them to love to read and write and be successful at it? Don't we want our students to be curious about how words work and develop strategies that work whether they are decoding words or spelling them? Wouldn't our job be so much easier and more enjoyable if students couldn't wait for word study each day?

My journaling, my reflections, and questioning led me to reconsider what I was doing with spelling and phonics. I wanted answers to my questions, and I found some when I started to look to existing research.

When I first started reading research and applying some of what I read, the results were not only encouraging, they spurred me to continue reading, to make further changes in my practice, and to share what I had learned with others. My students' excitement as well as their growth have been inspirational to me and, as a result, I enjoy teaching more.

You will get to delve into some of the research in the next section, and you'll find it easier than I did to start finding answers to your own questions about word study. Marcia's collected a lot of it in one place and made it more manageable for practitioners who are not yet familiar with the language of formal research.

As you start reading about the research that Marcia describes in Section 2, I encourage you to begin that inquiry process by reading thoughtfully, reflecting on what you see in your own classroom, and writing down your aha moments—your personal goals and your questions along the way. You, too, can (and should!) be a researcher. When you begin to approach teaching that way, you will find it an enjoyable and beneficial way to grow both you and your students.

In Section 3, I'll be back with some practical ideas for how to take the research and make it work for *you*, in your classroom. I am still on this learning journey, even as I write this book. Come, join me on this journey! I think you will be excited to see that you do not have to be satisfied with teaching practices that only reach some of your students. You will be inspired by your students' engagement and interest in how words work. Finally, the inquiry process will lead you to becoming your own researcher in your classroom—and that is a very exciting and beneficial way to approach your own professional growth.

SECTION 2

WHY NOT? WHAT WORKS?

Let Students Show Us What to Teach Them

MARCIA INVERNIZZI

Many teachers share Jennifer's dissatisfaction with their phonics and spelling instruction, but they don't know what else to do. They know that they must teach phonics and spelling if their students are to learn to read and write, but these word-level skills seem like uninvited guests at the dinner table. Teachers and administrators search and search for the "right" program that can teach their students how to spell and decode, but they're looking in the wrong place. Instead of looking to programs, educators need look no further than the students themselves. Not so hidden within students' uncorrected writing and spelling attempts is the key to understanding what to teach to whom, and when. Right there in front of our eyes, if we only knew how to see. Let me show you what I mean.

Figure 2–1 shows a writing sample from first grader Lea. Looking first to see what she *can* do, we see that Lea knows how to spell many high-frequency words (e.g., *my*, *going*, *the*, etc.) including words with

Figure 2-1 Lea's Invented Spelling

My favorite field trip

write about your favorite field trip!

My favoret feeld
Chrip was going to
the pool. It vwrus fun

short-vowel sounds (e.g., *it, fun*) and consonant digraphs (e.g., *the*). These are the spelling features she represented correctly. But if we interpret the features she attempted but did not represent correctly, we see that she needs instruction in long-vowel patterns (e.g., FEELD for *field*) and some consonant blends—especially those that make an /tʃ/ sound such as the sound associated with *ch*, as in *chair* (e.g., CHRIP for *trip*). We can know this because in the early 70s, while studying the early writing attempts of preschoolers, a Harvard linguist named Charles Read (1971) discovered that the spelling "errors" children made revealed a keen phonetic logic at the base of their letter choices, a logic based on their sensitivity to articulatory gestures, or movements, in their mouth as they pronounced words and letter names. He discovered, for example, that preschool children who knew the alphabet (but not much more) often chose the letter H to represent the /tʃ/ sound in a word like *chicken*, spelling it HKN. Why H? Because the letter name "aitch,"when pronounced, produces the /tʃ/ sound that occurs at the beginning of *chicken*, a sound that is clearly felt at the roof of the mouth just behind the teeth. Read's research showed that young children possess an intuitive knowledge of very detailed aspects of spoken English that they tacitly organize into categories defined by articulatory features, the manner and place the sound was formed in the mouth. Young children make judgments about phonological relationships between words and letters based on these articulatory features, just as Lea did when she spelled CHRIP for *trip*. In Lea's case, the sound of *chr* is articulated in much the same way as the beginning sound in *trip*.

The Logic in Spelling Errors

Read's 1971 study is often referred to as the Rosetta Stone of spelling research because it showed how to interpret children's invented spellings, spellings that were previously considered totally random or at best whimsical approximations based on flawed visual memory for letter forms. Just as the Rosetta Stone provided the key to deciphering ancient hieroglyphics, Read's research showed that instead of visual memory, phonetic sensitivity and logic were the driving forces behind students' early spelling attempts. About the same time of Read's discoveries, Henderson and his colleagues at the University of Virginia found further evidence of linguistic logic behind students' misspellings in the elementary grades and beyond. Like Read, Beers and Henderson (1977) found that students' uncorrected spelling attempts provided a window into their understanding of how English orthography, the correct spelling of words, represents pronunciations and meaning. They found that students' "errors" could be described linguistically as students advanced across the grades. The spelling errors of kindergartners and early first graders tended to cluster around the representations of speech sounds with letter–sound correspondences, like CHRIP for the /tʃ/ sound *trip* in Figure 2–1. In contrast, most second graders appeared to have mastered the basic phonics concepts related to letter–sound correspondences; their spelling errors tended to revolve around the use of *letter patterns* related to both sound *and* meaning—like whether the man mail carrier is spelled *male* or *mail*. Most spelling errors of students in the third and fourth grades clustered around issues related to the adding of suffixes that sometimes requires changing a letter, such as changing the *y* to *i* in words like *prettiness* or *babies*. While most achieving students in the upper elementary and middle grades appeared to have mastered these earlier spelling features, their errors revolved around Greek and Latin affixes and roots and how words related in meaning often share a similar spelling. Spelling researchers argued that understanding the logic behind students' spelling errors at different points in their development was essential for effective teaching of phonics and spelling and they set about creating resources to help (e.g., Bear et al. 2012; Flanigan et al. 2011; Ganske 2000).

In these early developmental spelling studies, not all students' spelling errors conformed to the predominant ones for their grade level, but even the spelling errors of students who were very advanced or very behind could also be described by these same linguistic features. For example, very young students who were precocious in their reading achievement made spelling errors typical of older students who often use but confuse homophonic pairs, spelling *routine* (from *route*) as *rootine* (from *root*), for example. Likewise, older struggling readers made spelling errors more typical of younger students who often use but confuse long-vowel patterns As a result, Henderson and colleagues concluded that rather than using rote visual memory, students acquire specific spelling features in a developmental progression that builds on language concepts related to sound and meaning, and that students use these aspects of language, combined with their current understanding of spelling patterns, in very predictable ways (Henderson 1990). Further, they stressed that children's understanding of English spelling fueled their learning in both reading and writing. Research has since established that the process of reading words, and the process of writing words, both draw from a common core of underlying *orthographic* or *spelling* knowledge that supports both (Ehri 1997; Perfetti 1997). Recent research in neuropsychology suggests that variations in how completely linguistic attributes of written words are represented in our heads has consequences for reading skill, including reading comprehension. That's because efficient and reliable retrieval of word meanings depends on accurate and complete representations of word features relating to speech sounds (*phonology*), spelling patterns (*orthography*), and word meanings (*semantics*) in memory (Perfetti 2007). Knowledge of how the spelling of words relate to sound and meaning allows for greater facility with reading and writing. By analyzing children's spellings, we can learn important information about their understanding of how written words work, understandings that shape the quality of their interactions with texts (Templeton 2007). Most importantly, we can use this information to differentiate the content of our phonics, spelling, and vocabulary instruction so that children can move to the next level in their literacy achievement. We need only look at what children know, as revealed in their spellings. In a sense, our study of children's developing word knowledge mirrors the kind of critical thinking about words we want our students to engage in during phonics and spelling instruction—looking for and expecting logic related to sound and meaning.

Student Diversity in Word Knowledge

As a new teacher, Jennifer was aware of the incredible variety in her students' personalities, backgrounds, and behaviors, and she went to great lengths to get to know her students and their families. But what she didn't know was exactly what each child already knew about English spelling and what they needed to learn next. At that point, she didn't yet understand how diverse student understandings of written words' representations of sound and meaning could be. This fact started to dawn on her when she realized that the students who always scored high on phonics worksheets were the same ones who already knew that phonics feature to begin with—an insight she gleaned from administering a pretest. But as useful as pretests are, they serve a limited purpose: they are designed solely to find out what students already know about the curricular materials you are about to give them. Pretests cannot provide the kind of diagnostic assessment needed to differentiate instruction. Qualitative spelling inventories, on the other hand, assess what students already know about a range of features characteristic of the entire spelling system, hierarchical progressions of phonics and spelling features that must be mastered to become a fluent reader and writer. Unlike pretests, which assess children's readiness of a given set of materials, qualitative spelling inventories assess children's developmental spelling knowledge that in large measure determines the quality of their reading and writing. While pretests assess prior knowledge of a restricted set of *specific words*, qualitative spelling inventories assess prior knowledge of the *spelling system*, the overarching principles that determine how spelling represents pronunciations, meanings, and use in general.

How to Assess Word Knowledge

Qualitative spelling inventories use word lists that represent an array of spelling features occurring across texts at different grade levels. By administering a qualitative spelling inventory, teachers can determine where students are along the developmental continuum of orthographic knowledge as well as exactly what they already know and what they need to learn next to move forward.

For examples of diagnostic assessment in action, see Section 3, page 55

Although there are a wide variety of qualitative inventories to choose from, they are all quite similar (Bear et al. 2012; Ganske 1999; Invernizzi, Meier, and Juel 2003; Schlagal 1989; Viise 1994). Typically qualitative spelling inventories are first scored for overall "power"—where each student falls in the developmental continuum and then for features—exactly which spelling features have been mastered and which should be taught next (e.g., Ganske 2000; Bear et al. 2012). Figure 2–2 shows Dona's spelling inventory administered in the fall of third grade. Can you eyeball where she begins to fall off?

The Primary Spelling Inventory in Figure 2–2 (Bear et al. 2012) shows that Dona has mastered all the basic letter–sound correspondences (that is, beginning and ending consonants, short vowels, most consonant blends, and consonant digraphs) but she "uses but confuses" long-vowel patterns. Although she has learned the silent *e* (*hope*, *shine*, and *blade* are all correct), she overgeneralizes the silent-*e* pattern in her spelling of *wait* (WATE), *coach* (COCHE), and *fright* (FRITE). All the more advanced features on the latter part of the spelling inventory are wrong and are less interpretable. Dona's spelling inventory tells us that teaching her short vowels would be a waste of time—but so would jumping to the later features such a consonant doubling. Without the foundational understanding of long and short vowels, Dona would not be able to grasp the principles of consonant doubling or e-drop;

Figure 2–2   Dona's Qualitative Spelling Inventory

Name: Dona		Grade: 2gl	Date:

1.	Fan	14.	Frite
2.	Pet	15.	Chool
3.	Dig	16.	Krole
4.	Rob	17.	wishis
5.	hoPe	18.	thorn
6.	Wate	19.	Showted
7.	gum	20.	SPoyuld
8.	Sled	21.	Growle
9.	Stick	22.	Therd
10.	Shine	23.	campt
11.	Grem	24.	Frise
12.	Blade	25.	claPing
13.	Coche	26.	Rideing

these orthographic conventions depend on an understanding of vowel sounds. Dona, like all students, will need instruction targeted to her current understanding of how the spelling system works—where she is in the spelling-learning trajectory. Whole-class instruction, which was Jennifer's initial strategy, cannot accommodate such differentiation.

Meeting Diverse Needs Through Differentiated Small-Group Instruction

While whole class instruction may give teachers the illusion of control, the instruction will be pitched to only a small minority of students. Most will be above or below the grade-level curriculum for phonics, spelling, and vocabulary. Indeed, just like reading levels, most classes contain a range of at least three developmental levels (Schlagal 2002). No wonder that Jennifer grew dissatisfied focusing on second-grade phonics elements—in any given second-grade classroom some students will already know short vowels while others may still be grappling with initial and final consonant sounds. Her observation that "students didn't seem to be learning anything they didn't already know" was right on. Her instruction was over the heads of many of her students.

A series of studies in elementary-grade classrooms (Morris, Nelson, and Perney 1986; Morris et al. 1995b; Morris et al. 1995a) proved the need to differentiate spelling instruction based on students' orthographic knowledge. The researchers found that undifferentiated, whole-group instruction was particularly ineffective for the bottom third of a class that could not spell even half of the words on a qualitative spelling inventory. Students who received differentiated spelling instruction on their developmental level (as opposed to grade level) scored higher on posttests of studied words, and even higher than the controls on unstudied transfer words from a level above them. The Morris et al. studies (1995a, 1995b) provide an evidence-based rationale for establishing levels for spelling instruction with qualitative spelling assessments and for differentiating instruction based on those assessed levels. Whether these levels are called *stages* (Ganske 2000; Bear et al. 2012) or *phases* (Ehri 2000), they all refer to the degree of student understanding of how the spelling system works to represent aspects of language—the sounds of language, nuances of use, and meaning. On the one hand, what students remember about specific word spellings is influenced by what they understand about the overall spelling system—how the spelling of words represents pronunciations and meanings in general. On the other hand, what students are able to learn about the overall spelling system develops partially from their accumulated experiences with specific word spellings (Ehri 2005). No wonder the Morris et al. studies (1986; 1995a; 1995b) found that students who received differentiated spelling instruction on their developmental level (as opposed to grade level) not only scored higher on posttests of the studied words but even higher than the control group on unstudied transfer words! Prior knowledge of how spelling works to represent sounds and meanings both facilitates and constrains the acquisition of new orthographic understandings.

Students learn when they make connections between their existing, prior knowledge, and the new knowledge to be acquired. When the content of word study instruction is targeted just beyond but not too far beyond students' existing knowledge base, students can integrate incoming knowledge with their existing schema for how written words work. Students understand and learn when the content of phonics and spelling instruction is within their *zone of proximal development.* The zone of proximal development has been defined as "the distance between the actual developmental level, as determined by independent problem solving, and the level of potential development, as determined through problem solving under adult guidance, or in collaboration with more capable peers" (Vygotsky 1978, 86). The first step in planning effective word study instruction is to ascertain students' "actual developmental level" in spelling knowledge by administering a qualitative spelling inventory. The second step involves organizing small groups for differentiated instruction.

Understanding Development

Determining students' actual developmental level requires both knowledge and know-how—knowledge of the hierarchy of English spelling features and know-how to plan and differentiate instruction. As mentioned earlier, develop-

For tips on organizing small groups, see Section 3, pages 58–60

mental research has documented the convergence of specific kinds of spelling errors at certain stages of literacy development. These errors cluster qualitatively around certain linguistic concepts and reflect students' uncertainty over specific phonics or spelling principles—in other words, in their zone of proximal development. What Jennifer needed was knowledge of her students' zone of proximal development, the information with which she could have then used to plan and differentiate instruction.

Students' spelling confusions relate to elements of sound, pattern, and meaning, three conceptual tiers of orthographic knowledge. Not to be confused with tiers of vocabulary learning or tiers of intervention in a Response to Intervention (RTI) framework, the conceptual tiers of orthographic knowledge relate to learning how the spelling of words relates to pronunciations and meaning. Errors in the first tier deal with the alphabetic match of letters and sounds (YN for *when*; SEP for *ship*). Errors in the second tier deal with letter patterns (BRANE for *brain*) and syllable patterns (TOPING for *topping*). Errors in the third tier concern how the spelling of words can cue their meaning (COMPUTITION for *competition*—not realizing that *compete* provides the clue to the correct spelling). The same clustering of error types has been noted among students with learning disabilities and dyslexia (Worthy and Invernizzi 1989), students who speak in variant dialects (Cantrell 2001), and students who are learning to read in different alphabetic languages (Helman 2004). Longitudinal research has demonstrated similar developmental progressions in error types for all learners of written English *varying only in the rate of progression* (Templeton 2007). These findings have profound implications for teaching *all* students. Instead of thinking of "outliers" as needing something "different," *all* students learning to read and write English experience these same developmental trajectories. Understanding their error types in relation to the scope and sequence of spelling features within and across these conceptual tiers provide the necessary insight for planning effective instruction for everyone. The fact that children progress through the tiers of orthographic word knowledge at different rates calls for ongoing assessment of student progress in spelling as well as continuous regrouping of students for instruction. The focus of instruction within these conceptual tiers of word knowledge is summarized in Figure 2–3, which should be read from the bottom up.

The Alphabetic/Sound Tier

Students negotiate the concepts within these broad tiers in stages or phases that loosely parallel their literacy development in general. Children are said to be at a certain stage or phase when most of their reading, writing, and spelling behaviors reflect the thinking characteristic of that stage. In reality, children may demonstrate a few behaviors from the next or previous stages. Children who have not acquired the *alphabetic principle* (tier 1) are considered *emerging* or *developing readers* who are still exploring the "big ideas" of literacy fundamentals such as a sense of story, word meanings, concepts about print, phonological awareness, alphabet recognition, alphabet naming, letter sounds, letter formation, concept of word, and so forth. Emergent readers have been called "pre-alphabetic" because they have not yet learned the alphabet or acquired the phonemic insight that alphabet knowledge and a concept of word affords (Flanigan 2007). Gradually, as these foundational concepts are learned, emergent readers become *beginning readers* whose spelling reveals a letter name–alphabetic logic to representing phonemes, at first partially (e.g., GF for *drive*), then more fully as they begin to learn more about phonics (e.g., GRIV for *drive*) and acquire an initial reading or sight-word vocabulary. The letter name–alphabetic logic used in these beginners' spelling can also be seen in the way they look at words in their reading, linearly and literally, letter by letter, sound by sound.

Figure 2–3 Instructional Focus by Conceptual Tier of Word Knowledge

Spelling Tier / Reading Stage	Typical Spelling	Typical Reading Error	Focus of Instruction
Meaning Tier / Advanced	• COLUM for *column* • PREPERATION for *preparation* • FRAGRENT for *fragrant* • CREDABLE for *credible* • SUCESSION for *succession* • IMMAGINERY for *imaginary*	• contemPLAtive for *comTEMplative* • deFIdence for *dIFfidence*	• Spelling–meaning connections • Greek and Latin roots • Latin-based suffixes and how they change part of speech • Common morphemes
Pattern-to-Meaning Tier / Intermediate	• STOPING for *stopping* • CATEL for *cattle* • NORMUL for *normal* • NACHURE for *nature* • ATTENSION for *attention* • PERTEND for *pretend*	• PILLOT for *pilot* • reFUSE for *REFuse*	• Inflectional endings (*-ing, -ed,* plurals) with spelling changes to the base word • Syllable patterns • Common affixes • Prefixes and suffixes

(continues)

Figure 2–3 (continued)

Spelling Tier / Reading Stage	Typical Spelling	Typical Reading Error	Focus of Instruction
Pattern Tier / Transitional	• CLEEN for *clean* • WATE for *wait* • SLOAP for *slope* • TRIE for *try* • STIKE for *stick* • CLOUN for *clown* • STAUL for *stall*	• GREET for *great* • DEED for *dead*	• Contrast short- and long-vowel sounds (pictures) and patterns (words). • Homophones • Inflectional endings (-*ing*, -*ed*, plurals) with NO spelling changes
Alphabetic Tier / Beginning	• H, HD, HID for *hide* • J, G, GRS, JRAS, CHRAS for *trash* • D, DG, DEG for *dig* • B, BD, BAD, BED for *bend* • P, PC, PK, PEK for *pick* • SC, SK, SAK for *sack* • D, DP, DOP, DUP, DOMP for *dump*	• HOT for hit • BAD for bed • WET for went	• initial consonant sounds (pictures) • consonant blends and digraphs (pictures and known words) • short-vowel sounds (pictures and known words) • preconsonantal nasals

Based on Bear et al. 2012

The Pattern Tier

Once students learn the basic array of phonics features (e.g., consonants, consonant digraphs, blends, and short vowels) and acquire a sufficient store of automatically recognized words, they begin to read independently and transition out of beginner books into simple chapter books like the Henry and Mudge series (Rylant) or *Fox on the Job* (Marshall 1988). These transitional readers spell most basic sound-based phonics features correctly; their errors now cluster around letter *patterns within words* (tier 2), patterns that include silent letters related to the sound of a different letter (e.g., NALE for *nail*; ROAP for *rope*). The linear alphabetic scan of the beginning readers doesn't work for silent letters, so transitional readers learn to consolidate these vowel patterns as orthographic "chunks." Chunking is more efficient and affords greater speed in word recognition, which in turn, allows silent reading (Invernizzi and Hayes 2012). As they devour series books like The Secrets of Droon (Abbott and Jessell), transitional readers learn to sustain reading for greater lengths of time and in a greater variety of genres. Before long, transitional readers acquire an extensive repertoire of long-vowel patterns in single syllable words, and their spelling errors begin to cluster around syllable patterns governing consonant doubling, e-drop, and other syllable patterns related to the addition of affixes. Called *syllable* and *affixes spellers*, these intermediate readers are typically reading books of considerable length, such as the Stranded series (Probst and Tebbetts) and later, literature such as the series His Dark Materials (Pullman). *Intermediate readers* learn to deconstruct longer words using structural analysis, removing prefixes and suffixes to focus on syllable patterns in base words.

The Meaning Tier

As students acquire an increasingly sophisticated vocabulary, they delve more deeply into the meaning or *morphological tier* of English orthography (tier 3), where spelling–meaning connections among related words provides the clue to spelling, parts of speech, and nuances of meaning (e.g., *heal–health–healthy*). Advanced readers in this highest stage of developmental word knowledge analyze how the sounds of consonants and vowels and consonants alternate among words derived from the same root (e.g., *crumb–crumble*; *decide–decision*). In addition to studying the constancy and change of spelling and pronunciation across derivationally related words, they study Greek and Latin roots and more sophisticated prefixes and suffixes, meaning units called *morphemes*. This level of word study is described as *generative*, because as students learn about spelling–meaning connections they are able to *generate* meanings for thousands of other words that share similar spellings or morphemes. For example, knowing the meaning of the word *recite*, and knowing that words related in spelling are often related in meaning, students can *generate* the meaning of *recital* and *recitation*, even if they hadn't studied those words. Figure 2–4 shows these tiers in relation to the content to be learned in phonics and spelling and phases of reading development. Qualitative spelling inventories, when combined with information about students' reading and writing, can help place students in this developmental continuum of instruction.

Developmental theories of spelling are useful because they provide a framework for the timing of instruction that match the particular needs of children. Students follow a predictable trajectory of literacy development, and teachers' understanding of this trajectory allows them to plan a curricular progression in synchrony with students' development and to differentiate the content of their phonics and spelling instruction. Appropriate word study instruction depends upon what concepts and features in the hierarchy of English orthography should be taught at specific points in time, relative to the child's developmental understandings (Invernizzi and Hayes 2012).

Developmental spelling theory is also a powerful tool for professional development. When educators understand how spelling develops, we are able to interpret our students' spelling attempts with linguistic insight and we are better equipped to move away from the old ineffective practices toward more engaging and effective language-based

Figure 2–4 Scope and Sequence of Phonics and Spelling Features According to Conceptual Tiers of Word Knowledge

Beginning and ending consonants	Short- vs. long-vowel sounds	Suffixes and prefixes
Consonant digraphs	Common long-vowel patterns	Sounded silent pairs (*bomb–bombard*)
Short vowels	Less common long-vowel patterns	Consonant alternations (*magic–magician*)
Consonant blends	R and l-influenced vowels	Vowel alternations (*compete–competition*)
Short-vowel patterns (CVC, CVCC, and so on)	Complex consonant patterns	Greek roots (*bio–biosphere, biography*)
Preconsonantal nasals	Ambiguous vowel diphthongs	Latin stems (*spect–inspector, disrespect*)
	Homophones and homographs	Predictable changes in related words (*explain–explanation, exclaim–exclamation*)
	Syllable patterns	Advanced suffixes (*-ence, -ance*)
	Inflectional endings (plural, past tense)	Assimilated prefixes

Based on Invernizzi and Hayes 2004

approaches. Armed with the conceptual foundations of developmental spelling theory, we are able see students' writing with fresh insight. What may have been thought of earlier as randomness or deficiencies of visual memory, children's spelling attempts are now interpreted according to the linguistic logic they represent. We become more attentive students of our students' writing and reading and begin to draw on invented spellings and word reading errors as diagnostic windows into students' understanding of how the written system works. Rather than seeing only what's missing or lacking, developmental spelling theory allows us to see what students are "using but confusing" and provide "just right" instruction to bring them forward.

Teachers don't need to be experts on English orthography to be effective in word study as long as they are willing to learn from and alongside of their students. True confessions: When I was still a classroom teacher I was asked, "Ms I., why do some words end in -*er,* some in -*ar,* and some in -*or* but they all sound like /ər/?" Not knowing the answer, I replied, "I don't know—let's see if we can find out!" As we collected, sorted, and talked about the words we found, one observant student remarked, "Hey! All of these -*er* words mean *more than*—like *fatter* is more fat than *fat*, and *taller* is more tall than *tall*!" Such was my own introduction to the power of learning alongside of my students and discovering the role of grammar in English spelling. While there are exceptions to any pattern in English (not all words ending in -*er* are comparative adjectives), the trick is to figure out which patterns are sufficiently common to be worth teaching. The best way to figure that out is by learning alongside of your students.

Debunking the Myths About English Spelling

Jennifer was also concerned about the lack of transfer from her phonics worksheets to more authentic tasks such as reading and writing. Of course, worksheets are not instruction and are isolated from actual reading and writing. An alternative is called *word study*, a conceptual, developmental approach to the teaching of phonics, spelling, and vocabulary.

Effective word study is more than just "word work" because it is rooted in the conceptual foundations of English orthography and timed in accordance with students' understanding of those concepts.

By now most people have heard the term *word study* and something called *word sorts*, but it's not as simple as having children write words on cards and push them around on a table. To design meaningful word study, it's important to have a conceptual understanding about the nature of the English writing system and how children learn to read and spell it. But part of acquiring the necessary knowledge about how English spelling works is debunking erroneous myths about the orthographic system.

Thanks to George Bernard Shaw and many others, English spelling has been unfairly maligned as being hopelessly irregular and, therefore, learnable only through rote visual memorization. Shaw used the example of the word *fish* spelled GHOTI to illustrate this point of view: GH makes the /f/ sound in words like *rough* and *tough*; O makes the short-*i* sound in words like *women* and the TI makes the /sh/ sound in words like *nation*. Of course what Shaw failed to consider was that in English, the spelling of a given sound varies by its position in a word (*gh* only sounds like /f/ at the end of words), that spellings sometimes preserve word origin in either sound or spelling pattern (*women*, from the Anglo Saxon *wyfman*), and that word meanings and parts of speech, such as the noun ending in *-tion*, trump simple phoneme–grapheme correspondences (*tion* only makes the /sh/ sound in morphemic contexts such as in the suffix *-tion*—*sh* is never used). Shaw thought English spelling was badly in need of revision and others still agree, as evidenced by ongoing protests of the Scripps National Spelling Bee by the Simplified Spelling Society.

> **For specific examples of how and when to use word sorts**
>
> see Section 3, pages 62–69

English Spelling Is Not as Irregular as You Might Think

One large-scale computer analysis of more than 17,000 words showed that nearly 85 percent of them were decodable based on sound-to-letter (phoneme–grapheme) correspondences, letter patterns, and predictable morphemes such as *-ed* and *-ing* (Hanna et al. 1966). In fact, it is estimated that as few as 4 percent of English words are truly irregular, and of them, only one is 100 percent irregular: *of*. The rest are at least partially regular (the word *from* is 75 percent predictable, for example) or explainable by word origin and history. Even the definition of *irregular* is colored by history. For example, the past tense of *lay* is *laid* and the past tense of *pay* is *paid*. So is the past tense of *say* really irregular after all? English spelling represents parts of speech (*syntax*) and word meanings in addition to speech sounds. While this results in a certain degree of complexity, it also allows for a greater economy of scale because English orthography conveys the meaning relationships among words. In fact, the great linguists Chomsky and Halle (1968) claimed that English orthography is "optimal" because it preserves in print what is otherwise obscured in pronunciation, such as the meaning relationship in derivational word pairs like *compete* and *competition*. The retention of the *e* in *competition* signals the meaning-based relationship to *compete* despite the fact that the long-*e* sound cannot be heard in the spoken word *competition* (pronounced com-*puh*-ti-tion). English orthography also conveys word meanings and word use within different contexts. For example, depending on the syllable stress, we can sign a *contract* to buy a new car (noun), or we can *contract* a virus from not washing our hands (verb). We can *speculate* (verb) that to *educate* (verb) our children will *translate* (verb) into better society.

Spelling Is Not Learned by Rote Visual Memory

Research also undermines the belief that visual memory is the best way to learn the spelling of words (Casar et al. 2005; Treiman and Bourassa 2000). First, there is the issue of *regular* words versus *irregular* words. Common sense would predict that if children primarily used visual memory to remember the spellings of words, then words with regular spellings (e.g., *fast*, *chest*) and words with irregular spellings (e.g., *bough*, *sure*) would be remembered equally well, provided they were otherwise equal in word length and frequency (Joshi et al. 2008). However, Treiman's (1993) research has shown that this is not the case. Children more easily remember predictable words, the words with regular phoneme–grapheme correspondences, suggesting that visual memory is not the only cognitive process involved in learning to spell. Second, there is the issue of visual-memory spans. Research has shown that children's visual memory for written spellings is limited to a span of two or three letters; therefore, visual memory cannot explain how children learn to read and spell longer words of four or more letters, much less words of multiple syllables (Aaron, Wilcznski, and Keetay 1998).

Several studies have compared visual memory to linguistic instructional approaches that emphasize how spellings relate to speech sounds (phonology), word meanings (semantics), and parts of speech (syntax). Arra and Aaaron (2001) found that the students taught with a linguistic approach outperformed those taught with a visual approach, which used flash cards. In a synthesis review of spelling instruction for students with learning disabilities, Graham (1999) found that the most successful approaches used a language-based approach that emphasized phonology and semantics. Berninger et al.'s (2000) research has also underscored the importance of making multiple connections between the linguistic aspects of spoken and written words, connections that teach the interrelatedness of sound, pattern, and meaning. In explaining the kind of spelling instruction that makes multiple linguistic connections Berninger and Fayo (2008) describe comparing and contrasting words with plural endings with other words without plural endings, as in words like *miss*, *cats*, *buses*, and *bees* (5). In thinking about how these words are the same and different, students must think about their ending sound (some end in an /s/ sound, some in an /is/ sound, some in a /z/ sound), the sound and spelling pattern of the base word, and their meaning (plural, not plural). Duke (in press) points out that we might spell *bugs* BUGZ, and *insects* INSEX if English orthography were based on sound alone (4). But since English is a morphophonemic orthography (that is, the

English spelling system represents both sound *and* meaning), we spell the ending of *bugs* and *insects* not by sound but with the morpheme *s* to indicate they are both plural.

While there have not been large, randomized control-group studies comparing various approaches to the teaching of phonics and spelling, there have been some smaller intervention studies that suggest that linguistic approaches that incorporate reflection and discussion on various aspects of language and orthography are not only superior in teaching students to spell specific words, but linguistic approaches also give students the knowledge to spell new words they had not yet studied. For example, Post and Carreker (2002) compared two instructional approaches for the teaching of the common suffix *-ion*, specifically whether to use *-sion* or *-tion*. The control group sorted words visually, according to whether the words ended in *-sion* or *-tion* with no discussion of the base words, word endings, or the sound of the *-ion* ending. The experimental group also compared and contrasted *-sion* and *-tion* words, but, in addition, these students were encouraged to notice and discuss the word endings in light of the sound and spelling pattern in the final syllable of the base word preceding the *-ion* endings. They discussed how the addition of the *-ion* endings changed the final sound of the base word in pairs like *produce–production* and *explode–explosion*. In *produce–production* the final sound of the base word changes from an /s/ sound to a /k/ sound, whereas in *explode–explosion*, the final sound of the base word changes from a /d/ sound to an /ʃ/ sound. The students in the experimental group, whose word study went beyond a sort of the visual patterns to include a rich discussion of the sounds, patterns, and meanings interacting between the base word and its derived *-ion* form, were not only able to spell the *-ion* words correctly, but they were also able to generalize the linguistic principles determining whether the base word took *-sion* or *-tion* to new words they had not yet studied— *reduce–reduction* and *divide–division*, for example.

Another study compared sorting word families like *ack* and *ake* by their visual array alone to an instructional approach that added student reflection and discussion. In this second condition, students thought about and discussed the sound of the vowels to puzzle out why some words ending in the /k/ sound ended in *ck* while others ended in *ke*. The latter group not only spelled more of the words correctly but they also read them more quickly (Post, Carreker, and Holland 2001). While certainly not conclusive, these results suggest that attention to and discussion of the linguistic aspects of written words—their sound, their spelling pattern, their meaning and use—is an important component of phonics and spelling instruction, and that visual-memory approaches devoid of language and linguistics are not as effective. Jennifer's concern about the lack of discussion about words and the rote nature of the tasks she assigned has been borne out by research.

Teaching for Transfer

When contemplating spelling instruction, teachers at all grade levels ask themselves questions about what words to teach, the number of words at a time, what to do with the very poorest spellers, not to mention how or when in a heavily scheduled day to fit in spelling. Though the need for some kind of spelling instruction is clearly evident in children's continual misspellings of even simple one-syllable words, as well as more complex multisyllabic words, teachers often have few workable strategies to employ in classrooms with students of varying abilities. To complicate matters further, teachers realize that decoding and spelling are intimately related and they are searching for ways to help children become more able readers. For lack of a better approach, many well-meaning and desperate teachers resort to the age-old practice of memorization. However, retention of words for spelling or reading dependent upon memorization alone is limiting because it assumes words are learned by rote, one at a time, like "adding beads on a string" (Templeton et al. 2015). That it does not work is proven over and over again when children misspell last week's words in this week's writing, or miscue a word they spelled correctly on a test last month.

In contrast what is needed is a way of exploring words that promotes thoughtful analysis of why words are spelled a certain way, a method that leads to *transfer*. Transfer in word knowledge occurs when students can use what they already know about how words work (no matter what level that might be) to explore and make connections to new levels of sound, pattern, and meaning. We need a method of spelling instruction and word study that facilitates transfer *and* enables students and their teachers to learn about words in ways that encourage problem solving at many levels, a much more lasting and useful cognitive strategy than rote memorization.

Ask, Don't Tell

Complex cognitive processes associated with problem solving cannot be imparted on a "just tell" basis. To truly teach for understanding, educators must devise a wider range of educational objectives for word study that are likely to result in both retention and transfer. Activities such as Guess My Category, word sorts, word hunts, and other variations of pattern detecting across sets of words, give students opportunities to think, analyze, and figure out how words work for themselves (Bear et al. 2012). The more opportunities children have to figure out things on their own, the more they start to believe that figuring things out is something they can do (Johnston 2004). When presented with contrasting sets of words, students can figure out the problem to be solved, then purposefully search for patterns of consistency. When students are not spoon-fed the answers, they make sense of things for themselves by analyzing and thinking critically about possible solutions. Our job is to "stack the deck" so that students *can* make sense of things. We do this by:

- Providing words that are developmentally appropriate to the students' zone of proximal development
- Presenting words that can be categorized into contrasting sets by sound, pattern, or meaning
- Exposing students to more cognitively demanding language through think-alouds, questions, and teacher talk that models

the cognitive processes of comparing and contrasting, analysis, hypothesis generation, and verification, and so on.

We promote problem solving by asking questions and provoking thoughtful analysis. In the two sets of words in Figure 2–5, what is the spelling question that begs to be asked? What do you notice that's the same about all of these words? But what's different between the two groups?

Figure 2–5 **What's the Question?**

pitch	teach
scotch	pooch
fetch	screech
ditch	reach

Teacher Talk for Promoting Thoughtful Analysis

Shallow tasks like memorizing flash cards, copying words five times each, or conducting word searches on mimeographed worksheets are not likely to engender deep conversations about word meanings, word use, how words sound, or how spelling is related to these linguistic components. That kind of spelling instruction is marked by lost potential; students could be doing more meaningful work with words. Effective word-study lessons pose questions and involve students in solving problems through intentional comparing and contrasting, thoughtful analysis, and discussion. Problems might be posed as questions, such as *Why do some words end in a* tch *and others in* ch*? Why do some words have a silent* e*? Why is there a* d *in* badge *but not in* cage*?* Critical questions such as these can spur an investigative mind-set and give purpose for engaging in instructional activities like word sorts. It also gives focus to important postsort reflections and discussion.

For specific examples of how to document students' understandings

see Section 3, page 58

The language we use when we talk with students has a powerful influence on students' sense of agency in learning and can engender a "growth mind-set" (Dweck 2007). This is as true of learning how to spell and read as learning anything else. Asking open-ended questions such as "What do you notice about these words?" and "Anything else?" can push children to notice more than one thing and suggests there are multiple aspects of words worth considering. When students ask how to spell a word as they are writing, asking, "What can you try?" conveys the message that there is more than one possible answer and puts student in the position to *select* a strategy and not just to use one (Johnston 2004). Providing feedback on what children have done partially correct ("I see you've gotten the first sound down. What comes next?") helps children notice what they are already doing right and develops self-efficacy (Bandura 1997; Clay 1993). Engaging students in looking and thinking about words encourages students to think about words flexibly and to integrate all that they are learning about the interdependencies among their sounds, patterns, and meanings. Figure 2–6 organizes some examples of teacher talk into language for problem solving, language for reflection, and language to encourage application and transfer to other words and other contexts.

Questions such as these ask students to take control of their learning and position themselves as word puzzlers (Scanlon 2011).

Critical Principles of Word Study

English spelling *is* complex, but it is also more logical and linguistically informative than most people think. Teachers can help students see that through thoughtful analysis of words they can figure out how the spellings of words work to represent not only pronunciations but meaning as well. By stacking the deck with appropriate words and spelling feature contrasts, teachers can help students achieve insight into the linguistically rich information represented in English spelling. In fact, teachers can help themselves achieve these insights right

Figure 2–6 Teacher Talk for Problem Solving, Reflection, Application, and Transfer

What do you notice about these words? How are they alike? How are they different from this set over here?	Tell me how it (the word hunt, the word sort discussion, and so on) went. What went well? What kinds of questions were raised? What were you sure of and/or unsure of?	What if we changed that *X* blend to a digraph (or a different blend)? What word would it be then?
Where in the word do you find the spelling pattern, root?	In your word hunt, which pattern did you find more frequently? Which pattern has the most words in the column? The fewest?	If you weren't sure how to spell a word with an *X* sound, how would you know which pattern to use? What would be your best bet? Why?
What are you noticing now? Any other patterns (or sounds) that surprised you?	What kind of pattern (or vowel sound or consonant blend, etc.) is this?	What if that word had a (long-*i* sound, and so on) in the middle? What word would it be then?
How else could you figure that out?	How did you figure that out?	Can you think of other words that have the same sound (or root, base word, and so on)?
What are some ways we could spell that word (or sound)? How could we check?	Why do you think it has that pattern?	One of the things people do when they aren't sure how to spell a word is to think of another word they know that either sounds like it (or that means the same thing). Let's try it. Let's say you don't know how to spell the word [____]. What other word might you think of that you do know?

(continues)

Figure 2–6 (continued)

Which part of the word are you sure about? Which part are you not sure about?	Do the word parts give you information about the word's meaning?	How else could you spell that word? What makes you think so?
Can you divide the word into parts? What is the base word? Are there any prefixes or suffixes?	Write down an observation about this word sort that you wish you had made.	
How are you planning to go about this (sorting or word hunting, or generalizing, and so on)?	What have you learned?	
	What problems did you come across in your word sort (or word hunt)?	

Based on Bear et al. 2014

alongside their students. Mindful word study builds on transactional, social-interactivist perspectives on language development, which assert that learning occurs as the result of dynamic interactions between children and their social contexts (Sameroff 2009). Transactional word study is based on the following ten guiding principles from *Words Their Way* (Bear et al. 2012, 87).

Look for what students "use but confuse"

This principle underscores the importance of teaching to students' zone of proximal development. Too often we want to teach to what our students don't know or what's not there, as if we can simply fill their empty heads with what they need. But we know that students understand and apply new knowledge when they build connections between the new and the old, when the new knowledge is integrated into existing schema. There is no existing schema if students are not at least attempting something. When we look for what students use but confuse, we look to see what they are attempting in their spelling but are not quite representing correctly. In Figure 2–7, the spelling attempts in the middle column show a student "using but confusing" long-vowel patterns. The spelling attempts in the right-hand column show a student who is not even attempting long-vowel patterns—all silent long-vowel pattern "markers" are missing. It is the student whose spelling is represented in the middle column who is ripe for word study instruction in long-vowel patterns.

Figure 2–7   Using but Confusing Long-Vowel Patterns

Correct (doesn't need instruction)	Using but Confusing (needs instruction)	Omitting Long-Vowel Patterns (not yet ready for instruction in long-vowel patterns)
ship	ship	sep
snake	snaik	snak
night	nite	nit
chewed	chood	chud
make	make	mak
leaf	leef	lef

A step backward is the first step forward

To integrate new knowledge into existing schema, it helps to "take a step backward" and contrast something new with something familiar. For example, students who already know short-vowel sounds in a variety of orthographic contexts (rhyming families, not in rhyming families, and so forth) are usually ready to study long-vowel spelling patterns. But what is a long vowel? The best way to find out is to contrast a long-vowel sound with the short-vowel sounds that are already familiar. A step backward is the first step forward. In the word sorts shown in Figure 2–8, students sort first by sound (a step backward), and then by pattern (a step forward).

Figure 2–8 A Step Backward Is the First Step Forward

First, Sort By Sound (a step back)			Next, Sort New Sound by Pattern (a step forward)		
short a	**long a**		**CVCe**	**_ai_**	
fast	face		face	rain	
black	rain		name	jail	
bath	name		made	paid	
ask	jail		came		
that	made		came		
	Take		take		

Many parents or teachers use a pretest–posttest framework to start word study on a new phonics or spelling feature. This makes good sense, with one refinement. Often the words that a student gets correct on the pretest are not included in the lesson—the teacher focuses exclusively on what the student got wrong. Including some words students already know how to spell (that follow the focal feature[s]) brings tacit knowledge to conscious attention. Including known words makes it possible for students to generalize the "old" to the "new" and apply their new awareness of pattern-to-sound and pattern-to-meaning relationships. Such a practice also exemplifies the principle "a step backward is a step forward."

Use words students can read

Learning to read and spell involves matching the orthography of printed words to their spoken counterparts and meanings. Making this connection is key to learning phonics, spelling, word recognition, and vocabulary. Unfortunately we often assume that students can analyze words they can't read by using new vocabulary words as spelling words, as Jennifer did when she assigned *cumulus*, *stratus*, and *cirrus*. We make the problem worse by trying to get students to analyze the spelling of the words they cannot even read in the unrealistic hope that they will see some sort of pattern or generalization. But if students don't know what the word is, they cannot make connections between its spelling and its pronunciation or meaning; students cannot analyze words they cannot read or understand. In contrast, when students can easily read and understand a word, they are able to consider its orthographic structure and compare it with other words they know that have similar sounds or meanings. When students are able to read the words they study, they are more likely to derive a generalization that may apply to other words with similar pronunciations or meanings. It's easier to look across words for consistencies in spelling patterns when the words are easy to pronounce.

Compare words "that do" with words "that don't"

It's easier to attach new labels to things that contrast greatly with one another than to things that are more alike (Treiman, Levin, and Kessler 2012). This basic learning principle applies as equally to learning to read and spell words as to learning the names of dinosaurs or ponies. To learn what a brachiosaurus is you have to see a stegosaurus or a tyranosaurus, not another brachiosaurus. What something *is* is in large part determined by what it *is not*, and this juxtaposition establishes a foundation that children continue to refine with additional experience. Children's uncorrected spelling attempts, along with the information gleaned from a qualitative spelling inventory, will suggest which spelling contrasts will help them straighten out their confusion. A child who spells *parties* as *partys* won't learn much by filling out a worksheet where all the examples change the final *y* to an *i* before adding *es*. Instead, compare and contrast a variety of words ending in *y* and discuss the spelling contexts associated with each pattern. Such a discussion will involve deconstructing the base word, if there is one, and observing the spelling pattern prior to the final *y*. Figure 2–9 compares and contrasts words ending in *y* with words ending in *ey* or *ay*.

Figure 2–9 Comparing Words That *Do* with Words That *Don't* (change the *y* to *i* before making plural)

Do		Don't	
funny	funnies	alley	alleys
fairy	fairies	jockey	jockeys
berry	berries	donkey	donkeys
body	bodies	chimney	chimneys
city	cities	pulley	monkeys
copy	copies	Friday	Fridays

In comparing words that do with words that don't, children are able to see recurring letter patterns within a group and recognize them as a *set*—they become aware of the *consonant + y* pattern at the end of words as a member of one set and the *vowel + y* words as members of another set. Grouping words into contrasting "sets" also makes them easier to remember and easier to write. Each set contains shared graphic components that can be produced in a similar way. As children compare words that do to those that don't, they begin to distinguish what's the same and what's different, and to map those spellings onto pronunciations, meanings, and even movements in writing. In the previous example, students will begin to generalize a bigger principle at work that will allow them to read and spell other "*y* words" not yet studied.

Sort words by sound, sight, and meaning

This principle reflects the importance of engaging students in thinking flexibly about words. Consider the words *hit*, *bike*, *give*, *crib*, *mice*, and *shine*. If asked to sort these words by sound, the word *give* would be grouped with *hit* and *crib*. If asked to sort these words by sight, *give* would go with *bike*, *mice*, and *shine*. In these two different approaches, *give*, a high-frequency word, is considered in more purposeful and flexible ways. Too often, we ask students to memorize visual patterns at the expense of how words sound or what they mean. The word sorts in Figure 2–10 illustrate just a few ways in which meaning also plays a role in spelling. Both sound and visual patterns are integrated into students' knowledge of word meanings through the orthography.

Figure 2–10   Sort Words by Sight, Sound, and Meaning

tax	tacks	made	maid	grow	grew	grown
ad	add	mane	main	throw	threw	thrown
an	Ann	male	mail	blow	blew	blown
		stare	stair			

In the group of contrasts on the left, word meanings dictate the spelling pattern, not pronunciation. Since *male* has one meaning (boy, man), the *mail* referring to cards, bills, and letters must have a different spelling pattern to tell it apart. The sort on the right contrasts an underappreciated aspect of meaning: parts of speech. How wonderful to discover the constancy and change in spelling among verb forms!

Begin with obvious contrasts first

When students begin the study of a new phonics or spelling feature, it's best to choose key words or pictures that are easily distinguishable, both visually and phonologically. For example, when teaching beginning consonants, it is best not to begin by contrasting *b* with *p*, which are both made with the lips, or with lowercase *d*, which also looks quite similar. Better to begin by contrasting *b* with something totally different at first—*s*, for example—before working toward finer distinctions. Likewise, in teaching letter–sound correspondences, it is best not to contrast *c* with *k* at first, since they both have a /k/ sound. Of course children do have to learn that the /k/ sound can be made with either letter, but in terms of linking the visual shape of a letter, its name, and its sound, *c* would be better contrasted with something totally different—*f* or *d*, for example. It's best to move from general, gross differences to finer discriminations over time. Research has repeatedly demonstrated that letters that are visually and phonologically confusing (such as *b/d, j/g/, y/w*) are among the most difficult to learn (Huang and Invernizzi 2012).

Don't hide exceptions

Words that seem to be an exception from one point of view might follow another pattern of consistency (yet to be discovered) from another point of view. Consider once again the high-frequency word *give*. It is true that *give* does not follow the pronunciation of other CVCe long-*i* spelling patterns, so in this sense it is an "exception." But when encountering other words like *glove, love, have*, students might notice the *v* in all of them and after hunting for other vowel-*v*-*e* words come to discover that no word in English ends in a *v* without an *e* (except *Luv* diapers!). Instead of hiding these exceptions, place these so-called irregular words in a miscellaneous or oddball category. New categories of consistent patterns sometimes begin to emerge. For example, after sorting two different double-*o* categories by sound (the long-*u*-like sound /ooo/ in words like *root* and *soon* versus another vowel sound made in the back of the mouth in words like *wood* and *foot*), students might encounter *could, would*, and *should* and consider them exceptions since they have the same sound as in words like *wood* and *foot*. Setting those words aside as oddballs will reveal a consistent pattern across all three and discovering this small but consistent pattern will make this set of high-frequency words more memorable. Of course *wood* and *would* are also *homophones* (e.g., words pronounced the same) and present a convenient opportunity to discuss the necessity of having different spelling patterns to reflect their different meaning. There are, of course, some words that really are exceptions (*was*, **laugh**), but these become more memorable by noticing their uncommonness in contrast to other words that share similar spelling patterns (e.g., **has**, *cause*, and so on).

Avoid teaching with rules

Rules are useful mnemonics if you already understand the underlying concepts at work, but they are not useful teaching tools. If the rule "When two vowels go walking, the first one does the talking" seems worthwhile to you, it is probably because you already know a lot of examples that follow that rule (e.g., *main, team, road*). A basic principle of learning is that we need to be familiar with a good number of examples before the rule that explains those examples can be detected, but when it comes to spelling instruction, we are often guilty of reversing this basic principle of learning. Not only is it necessary to have already been *able* to read and spell a good number of examples before the rules will make sense, but some rules are just not that useful anyway (Johnston 2001). The above-cited rule is often broken in words like *bread*, *root*, or *boil*, so in reality, this rule teaches children nothing. Students must learn to consider sound and pattern simultaneously to discover pattern-to-sound consistencies, and they must know a number of examples before they can generalize the principles at work. Generalization requires practice and experience in analyzing and discussing words, comparing and contrasting them by various attributes related to sound, pattern, and meaning. With guidance, students can discover consistencies and make generalizations for themselves. For example, students might record their word sorts in a word-study notebook and explain, in their own words, why they grouped the words as they did as shown in Figure 2–11. Our job is to structure categorization activities that reveal these consistencies and to encourage students to notice, ask questions, and search for order. Rules might help consolidate understandings, but they are no substitute for experience.

Figure 2–11 Word Study Notebook

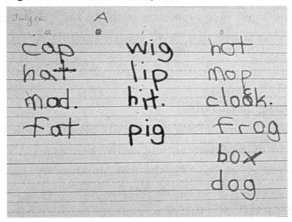

Work for fluency and flexibility

As students become more adept at sorting known words into categories by different criteria, they move from "hesitancy to fluency" (Bear, Negrete, and Cathy 2012) and from rigidity to flexibility. At first, students must examine each word quite deliberately to decide in which category it belongs. But one sort is not enough. Multiple opportunities to sort and discuss the thinking behind their sorting decisions not only results in the more routine application of strategies, but these strategies also become more flexible over time. Students begin to consider not just sound but *also* pattern. They begin to consider not just sound and pattern, but sound, pattern, *and* meaning. Acquiring automaticity in sorting and flexibility in thinking about sound, pattern, *and* meaning leads to the cognitive fluency needed for proficient reading and writing (Cartwright et al. 2010). With greater automaticity and flexibility also comes a greater sense of agency and independence; students can more easily go beyond what we teach them to generalize to new words and new meanings (Johnston, Ivy, and Faulkner 2011).

Link word study to reading and writing

If we want our students to connect what they are learning in word study to reading and writing, then we must help them do so. One way to do this is to keep a running list of word recognition errors students make in their oral reading in their guided reading groups to look for broad, orthographic concepts these errors may represent. Later on, these errors can be revisited. For example, if students stumble on the words *agreed*, *seed*, and *wheel* in a guided reading lesson, these words can be written on a dry-erase board or chart after the reading and re-visited. The teacher might ask students to consider their vowel sound and then to look to see if there is any commonality in the representation of that vowel sound in the words *seed* and *agreed*. Observations about the *ee* pattern might be applied to *wheel*, and the teacher might ask students if they can find another word on a certain page that also has a long-*e* sound spelled with the *ee* pattern (like *peel*).

Revisiting texts already read or written to look for words that contain similar sounds, spelling patterns, or spelling–meaning connections is called *word hunting*. Word hunting and the reflection and discussion that emanates about the words that are found demonstrate the utility of word study in actual reading and writing contexts. Students see that the spelling patterns they are studying have relevance to the words they read and write. In addition, word hunting "extends the reach" by allowing students to transfer and apply what they are learning in word study to other less controlled contexts. Very often these less controlled contexts contain more difficult words. For example, after sorting one-syllable short- and long-*e* words into categories headed by the words *best*, *keep*, and s*cream*, a student might add the words *asleep*, *canteen*, and *proceed* to the *keep* (long *e* spelled *ee*) column, and the words *retreat*, *mislead*, and *defeat* to the *scream* (long *e* spelled *ea*) category. Hunting for words in already read text provides the opportunity to extend the pattern-to-sound consistencies of one-syllable words to more difficult two-syllable words. Word hunting encourages students to transfer and apply their growing word knowledge to more complex words and to generalize to other contexts.

In addition to word hunts, there are many fun and engaging trade books that build on various aspects of word knowledge such as homophones (*Dear Deer* [Barretta 2010]; *The King Who Rained* [Gwynne

1988b]; *A Chocolate Moose for Dinner* [Gwynne 1998a]); eponyms (e.g., *Guppies in Tuxedos* [Terban 2008]; *Anonyponymous: The Forgotten People Behind Everyday Words* [Marciano 2009]); idioms (*Punching the Clock and Funny Action Idioms* [Terban 1990]; *In a Pickle* [Terban 2007a]), and other forms of figurative language (*Mad as a Wet Hen* [Terban 2007b]). So much of reading comprehension hinges on an understanding of figurative language, as in this sentence: "The trees stood still as giant statues" (from Jane Yolen's *Owl Moon* [1987]).

These ten principles of word study illustrate what Bear et al. (2012) call the "golden rule" of word study: *Teaching is not telling* (James 1958). Instead, students must have daily opportunities to examine, analyze, and categorize the spellings of words; reflect on their observations; orally discuss; and then test out their hypotheses about why words might be spelled as they are. Teachers make this possible by identifying students' stage of spelling and expanding their capacity to think and reason about increasingly more difficult word features within their zone of proximal development. By matching the content of English spelling to the developmental knowledge of the learner, teachers can devise word study lessons that focus students' attention on critical contrasts that reveal the deeper structures of sound, pattern, and meaning, the fundamental principles that determine the surface structure of individual word spellings.

For examples of grounding word study in meaningful reading and writing

see Section 3, pages 70–76

Purposeful word study goes beyond the mere retention of the surface structures of individual word spelling. While the retention of individual word spellings is important, retention of surface structures alone is insufficient to transfer to new words, to generalize to entire sets of words, or to understand how the spelling system works so that new words may be read or written. To teach for understanding, teachers must connect word study to reading and writing in meaningful ways and talk with and listen to children as they share their observations and thinking.

Spelling and Vocabulary: What's the Link?

Jean Chall (1983) observed that the vocabulary in children's textbooks changed at about the fourth-grade level, shifting from mostly familiar words that exist in children's speaking vocabulary to more unfamiliar and abstract content-specific or academic word meanings that exceed their oral vocabulary knowledge. Chall attributed the national decline in reading achievement scores at the fourth-grade level to students' lack of exposure to information and vocabulary. She believed that even students who could read would be unable to comprehend what they read without a critical mass of background knowledge and vocabulary. She called this state of affairs the "fourth-grade slump."

Emphasize Spelling–Meaning Connections

Chall's observations made so many years ago still hold true today: early gains in test scores from emphasizing phonics and spelling are not sustained when the vocabulary load increases. However, we can increase children's vocabulary knowledge and, consequently, their reading comprehension when we build on spelling–meaning connections among related words. Words that share similar meanings often share similar spellings even if the pronunciation changes across derivational forms (Templeton et al. 2010). Spelling–meaning connections can be seen in word pairs such as *invite* and *invitation.* In *invitation,* the *i* is retained to link to the meaning of the base word *invite,* even though the sound of the second *i* changes from a long-vowel sound in *invite,* to an "uh" or schwa sound in *invitation.* These morphophonemic aspects of related word forms can generalize to thousands of words that work the same way (e.g., *combine–combination*; *define–definition,* and so on). Within this kind of instructional framework, students consider words as a detective might; as students work with different forms of words that are related in meaning, they learn to figure out the meanings of words they've never seen before.

Because more than 60 percent of English vocabulary and more than 90 percent of vocabulary in the sciences is created through a combination of Latin and Greek roots, prefixes, and suffixes, knowing how these Latin and Greek roots and morphemes combine to make new but related words can significantly increase vocabulary knowledge and positively impact reading comprehension. Instead of teaching vocabulary one word at a time, teachers can teach the meaning *system* revealed in English spelling by grouping words that share the same base word or root. For instance, words related to the number two (*bi-*), such as *bicycle*, *biweekly*, and *bilingual*, can be grouped and compared to words related to the number three (*tri-*), such as *tricycle*, *triceratops*, or *triangle*. When generative word study of this nature is connected more specifically to ideas and themes in the texts students read, the result can be an exponential growth in academic content-area vocabulary and comprehension (Baumann 2009).

Of course not all students have the developmental spelling knowledge to profit from the study of spelling–meaning connections just described. If they are working to learn the features within the alphabetic tier, students won't be able to read, much less spell, words such as *cirrus* and *cumulus*, as Jennifer had hoped. Not only were these words developmentally inappropriate for students like Malina (who couldn't even read them), but they were not grouped within sets that shared any sort of spelling–meaning connection either. These words were not retained in memory because they couldn't be read and there were no common spelling patterns to grab on to when moving from word to word. Looking such words up in the dictionary isn't really possible when you can't read and don't know how to spell the word in the first place.

Offer Parallel Instruction in Morphological Awareness

An alternative described by Templeton et al. (2015) is to maintain a process of parallel instruction in *morphological awareness*, in which teachers build awareness of morphemes—word units that carry meaning such as prefixes and suffixes and high-frequency roots—even in the early grades and in the earlier tiers of spelling development.

Morphological awareness is becoming aware of the forms and structures of words that carry meaning, such as inflectional endings that signal number and tense (hug*ged*, hug*ging*, hug*s*), derivational endings that change part of speech (luck–luck*y*; color–color*ful*), and prefixes such as the *re-* (*again*), in *re*do, *re*fill, or *re*pay, or the *un-* (*not*) in *un*able, *un*real, or *un*like. When students learn even a simple word like *help*, they might also learn how to "build and extend" that word to others that contain the same base by adding simple high-frequency affixes (Flanigan et al. 2011). Instead of just learning *help*, students might also learn *helpful, helping, helpless, unhelpful,* and so on. Instead of teaching one word at a time, we can teach entire sets of words; instead of learning one word, students can learn ten. Students learn more when they make spelling–meaning connections among several words in a group. Recognizing even one or two familiar morphemes in an unfamiliar word can unlock its meaning.

Emphasize Multiple Meanings

The power of word study is also boosted when we emphasize the *polysemy*, or multiple meanings, of words. Almost all words have multiple meanings and calling students' attention to this can link phonics and spelling instruction to vocabulary learning. Even simple words have multiple (and often metaphoric) meanings (Nilsen and Nilsen 2004). Consider the word *leg*, a simple word that might appear in a word sort designed to teach the spelling of the short *e*, a word that also has multiple meanings:

- I have two *legs* to stand on.
- The horse took the lead in the final *leg* of the race.
- Organizing a party takes a lot of *leg*work.
- He's pulling your *leg*.

Every word sort designed to teach a phonics or spelling feature has the potential to expand vocabulary by calling attention to, explaining, and discussing the multiple meanings of words. Of course it would be tedious to do this for every word, but discussing the multiple meanings of even just one or two words per lesson would expand the construct of word study from simple "word work" to a more robust model of word study that integrates phonics and spelling with vocabulary instruction. By simultaneously taking advantage of the multiple meanings of words, students can develop a more nuanced understanding of word meaning, understandings that are essential to reading comprehension. Nevertheless, students will need a variety of rich encounters and experiences with words before they can absorb their meaning and make them their own. And to provide those rich experiences, teachers will need to engage in an iterative process of assessing students' current zone of understanding to continuously adjust and refine their instruction. By continuously looking for what their students are "using but confusing," teachers will learn alongside of them as they "sort things out" together.

Some Final Thoughts

Through word study, students examine, manipulate, and categorize sounds, letters, spelling patterns, and morphemes within and across sets of words. As we reflect with our students about how the spelling of words works to represent both pronunciations and meanings, our word knowledge grows with theirs, and our insights about the synchrony of literacy development is deepened. The hands- and minds-on approach described in the next section motivates students to look for patterns of consistency within words that share the same sound or meaning, and helps them to generalize those insights from the specific words they have been studying to other words they may not yet have encountered. In this way, word study generates the word knowledge that undergirds reading and writing, and in the process, nurtures a kind of flexibility in thinking. To get a better vision of what this all looks like in practice, let's move to the next section.

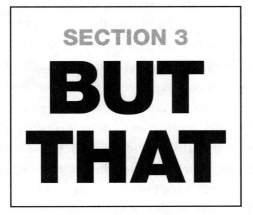

SECTION 3

BUT THAT

Deep Engagement With Words

JENNIFER PALMER

How do you as a teacher use this research regarding effective phonics and spelling instruction? You'll change and grow as I did, one step at a time. Set a goal. Try one or two of the practices outlined in this section. When you feel ready, try some more. Take time to study, think, and experiment. With a colleague or two, spend half an hour each week discussing how students learn phonics and spelling in your classroom.

What Are Students Ready to Learn?

To teach in a way that ensures every student is learning, you need to address word learning as a developmental continuum. Research shows that a one-size-fits-all approach to phonics and spelling doesn't work. Think about the students you have right now. Some of them misspell words that have suffixes. Some have mastered the short vowels but put a silent *e* on everything with a long vowel. Still others use an *a* for all short vowels. A few may just string consonants together without any vowels at all. There's a wide range of abilities and needs in every class.

The key is to match your instruction to developmental spelling levels. To identify a student's spelling ability, you need a strong diagnostic tool. I use the *Words Their Way* (Bear et al. 2012) inventories and Richard Gentry's (2007) Monster Test (ten words dictated to students, much like a traditional spelling test). The Monster Test is a good place to start if you have never used inventories before; it's easy to use and score and will help you decide where to begin your instruction. The *Words Their Way* inventories and Kathy Ganske's Developmental Spelling Assessment (2013) provide more detailed information about spelling levels, and their creators include a thorough explanation of students' developmental readiness and instructional activities to try, at each level. The assessment tool you choose will reveal a great deal of information about your students.

What the Right Assessment Tool Can Reveal

One of Gentry's Monster Test words is *bumped*. A child who spells this *bumt* is able to hear most of the sounds in the word and use appropriate letters for those sounds. In order to spell the *-ed* suffix correctly, he must understand that *-ed* carries meaning; it's a *morpheme*, the smallest meaningful unit in English, and it makes a verb past tense. It's also a *bound* morpheme (it cannot stand alone). Words with an *-ed* suffix sometimes have a consonant /t/ sound at the end, as *bumped* does. Eventually students understand that a word with an *-ed* ending representing past tense may sound as if it should be spelled with a *t* but is spelled with an *-ed*. A child who is able to use the *-ed* bound morpheme at the end of a word rather than a phonetic spelling is at a more advanced developmental level.

By administering a spelling inventory several times a year, you'll learn a great deal about how student spelling develops. For example, a student's spelling of *bumped* may progress from BP (no vowels represented) to BOPT (a short vowel in place and a letter for every sound except the consonant cluster *mp*) to *bumped* (conventional spelling). If she also spells *united* as YOUNIGHTED, you have more evidence that she has moved away from just matching letters to sounds. This is an important step. A student who is using but confusing certain vowel patterns/meaning units is ready to start learning them.

Comparing Encoding and Decoding Skills

For a chart of spelling development

see Section 2, pages 23–24

Decoding skills are the other side of the spelling coin. They're often a bit ahead of encoding skills—students can usually read more words than they can spell—but comparing students' spelling mistakes with their word recognition errors captured on running records (a system for coding the miscues students make as they read orally) lets you see patterns in students' thinking about reading and spelling—connections and overlaps between the two—that help you know what to teach next. See Figure 3–1.

Figure 3–1 Running Record

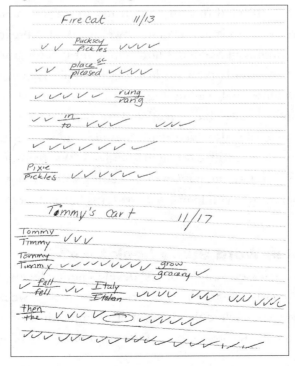

(You can gather information similar to that of a running record by writing down the word a student missed and how the student pronounced it.) This process is also a great way to understand more deeply how reading and writing are interconnected.

Students often use but confuse things in their reading and writing, but once they can decode a particular pattern accurately and consistently, they quickly learn to spell the pattern. First grader Karen is a great example. One day as she was reading aloud with me, she kept pronouncing the word *tape* as "tap-ee," then scowled and tried again. Eventually, using the sentence context, she figured out the word was *tape*. She asked me why there was an *e* at the end of *tape* since it didn't make a sound. I gave an impromptu lesson on the silent *e*, knowledge she applied the next day when she encountered the word *pine*. However, in her writing she started putting a silent *e* on the end of every word with a long *a* sound, a perfect case of using but confusing that vowel marker. The *Words Their Way* inventory I administered a couple of days later confirmed that she was ready to start comparing words with long-vowel sounds to the short-vowel words she already knew.

Marcia mentions in Section 2 how important it is for students to be able to read the words they are learning to spell. Systems for taking notes on students' oral reading (e.g., running records) show us which words they are already able to read and are therefore a good source of information as we decide which words they are ready to study. For example, students who are still learning to sound out CVC (consonant-vowel-consonant) words like *cut* or *rot* in their reading will certainly struggle to read and spell words with long-vowel patterns like *cute* or *throat*.

What Does Word Study Look Like?

Once you've assessed your students' developmental levels, what next? Maintain a consistent routine—either three times a week or every day, whatever your schedule allows. For example, in first and second grade, you might devote thirty to forty minutes a day of word study, during which students participate in activities like word sorts, which is a valuable investment. Depending on your time constraints and students' needs, you can choose from the following suggested activities and groupings.

Creating Groups

Small-group instruction allows for thoughtful, flexible differentiation. Word sorts are a wonderful way to get students thinking, but how do you decide who to put in what group for what sort? How do you manage several groups of students learning different patterns? Here are a few things to consider:

1. Base groups on needs revealed by your spelling inventories and decoding observations, not convenience. (Word-study groups will very likely be different from reading groups.)
2. Carefully teach routines and procedures for what students should do when their group is *not* with you.
3. Design activities that are engaging (not just entertaining) and that develop student's understanding of words.

The students within a particular group should work on patterns they are ready to learn. Every group doesn't have to be the same size. Even though it may be easier to have three groups of eight, it may be better to have one group of four, a larger group of thirteen, and a third group of seven if that's how students' developmental levels compartmentalize. (For practicality's sake, the large group of thirteen may be broken down into a group of six and a group of seven when you work with them directly.) It's also possible for a student to be a group of one. If this seems tough to manage, don't worry: here are a few tips for managing word-study groups with routines and procedures.

For an understanding of the diversity in children's word knowledge

see Section 2, pages 16–17

Setting Up Work Stations

During small-group phonics and spelling instruction (word study), students have to be able to manage their time productively while you are working with another group. One approach is to set up several work stations (one of which you lead, in an area at the front of the room where you can keep an eye on things) and teach students the routines for each station and how to move from one to the next.

You could use work stations to:

- introduce and teach the rules of a new word study game
- administer a formal assessment
- record anecdotal notes about student progress (see Figure 3–2).

Figure 3–2   Teacher Note-Taking

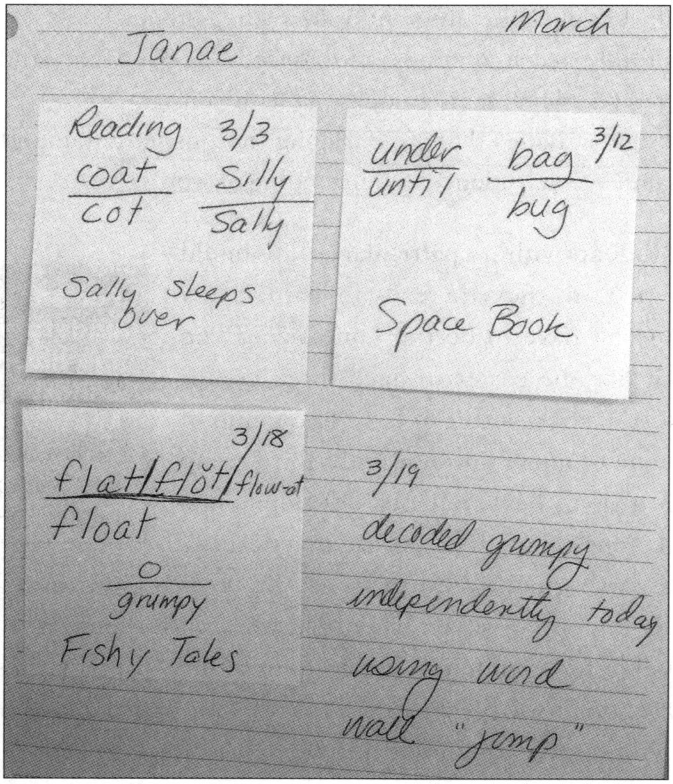

Another station might contain card games or board games matched to the pattern(s) students are studying. I use a table with a big plastic bin or bucket in the center for the games, which are stored in large ziplock bags labeled with the game name and color-coded (red games for word patterns, blue games for affixes, and so forth).

Word hunt stations are easy to manage. Here students transfer their knowledge of studied patterns by looking for words that include the patterns in texts *they have already read* and recording them in a notebook. Using familiar texts ensures that students will be able to read most of the words they find. Students can't hunt for words if they're struggling to read for meaning. Students record the title of the text they are hunting in at the top of a notebook page; underneath they list each word they find and the number of the page on which they found it. I sometimes give younger children or students just beginning word study a three-column sheet (see Figure 3–3) to glue into their notebook:

Figure 3–3 Word Study Template

Cat	Cake	Oddballs
ask at	tape ate	Art

The oddballs category is for words that follow a spelling pattern but don't have the right sound. In the example above, the word *art* does follow the regular pattern for an *r*-controlled *a*, but a student who is not familiar with *r*-controlled vowels and notices that *art* does not sound like *ask* and *at* might label it odd. This is an opportunity to start a conversation with that student and his group about a new pattern. The open-ended nature of a word hunt gives students a lot of control over their own learning, building a sense of agency—"I can do it!"—and cluing you into what kids might be noticing about words on their own. The difference between this and a worksheet is that the questions are open-ended, informed solely by the individual students' line of inquiry.

Other stations could simply be practice stations where students repeat sorts they have done under your guidance or reread a poem or decodable text containing the pattern being studied to a buddy.

I don't introduce all my stations on the same day. I teach the whole class how to work in one station at a time, and we practice following the rules for that station, maintaining an appropriate voice level, and moving to and from the station. I introduce the station I'm leading last, after I'm sure students can manage their behavior at the other stations independently. I also ask them to keep to a three-before-me policy: if they have a question, they must ask three other students before they ask me. I tell them my teaching time is precious and unless they are bleeding or their pants are on fire or someone is hurt or sick, I am not to be interrupted. Students laugh about the pants-on-fire scenario but it helps them understand that they should try to solve any problems they have on their own before intruding on my work with a group. Turning responsibility for their learning over to the students creates the culture I want, one in which everyone works together and everyone helps one another.

Debriefing

At the end of each word study session I ask students to sit together on the rug in our classroom and talk about how it went. This discussion is very brief (five minutes) but it keeps students accountable and productive.

I end this discussion by having students share what they learned with a partner or by calling on a student from each group to share with the class. Talking about what they've learned lets students practice using language to describe word patterns and feeds their interest in how words work. Debriefing sessions often take longer when you are beginning to use work stations, but they get shorter and shorter as students become accustomed to the routine.

There are some important advantages to a work-stations approach. Being able to move from one station to another helps young, active children stay focused. Working together creates opportunities for productive student-to-student conversations about words. If you take the time to model how to work at stations and remind students about routines and procedures every day, even kindergartners can manage their time productively. A word study session with four stations might include:

Figure 3–4   Word Study Configuration

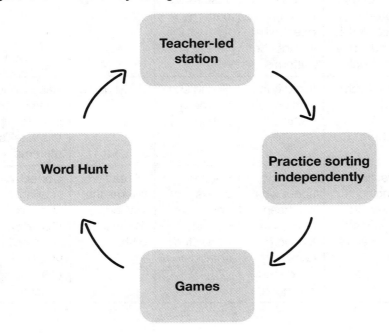

Alternative Configurations

You could also give all students the same daily word study activity, varying the words appropriately for the various groups. The activities need to be modeled carefully and practiced consistently throughout the year. Figure 3–5 is just one of many possible configurations of a series of whole-class word study activities. (The activities are described in more detail later in this section.)

This approach is particularly good in crowded classrooms in which the traffic patterns required with rotating stations are hard to orchestrate. The varied routines—sorting, writing, hunting for words, and reading words containing the patterns—allow students to recognize

Figure 3–5 Whole-Class Word Study Configurations

Monday	Tuesday	Wednesday	Thursday	Friday
Teacher-led word sort of new pattern, recorded in word study notebook	Practice yesterday's sort by reading poems that include the pattern	Word hunt for yesterday's pattern	Blind sort	Quiz or blind sort
Word game reviewing previous pattern	Word game with new pattern	Speed sort of weekly patterns	Word game	Read aloud poems that include this week's patterns
Practice reading poetry that includes last week's patterns	Write about what has been learned in the word game in word study notebook	Record words from word hunt in word study notebook	Reread poems that include this week's patterns	Correct spelling errors of this week's patterns in pieces in their writing folders

and use the patterns in many different contexts, thus increasing the likelihood that the knowledge will transfer from one context to the next. Teacher-led sorts should still be conducted in small groups, however, with each group working with words or patterns appropriate to their spelling level.

For the research that supports word sorts

see Section 2, page 32

Word Sorts

Whether you choose a work-stations approach or a daily structured routine, students can participate in many productive activities in each format that will keep them engaged and learning. In a word-sort activity students are given words on small cards or pieces of paper and asked to group them by categories. Word sorts encourage students to look for visual, aural, and/or semantic patterns depending on how the sort is designed. See Figure 3–6.

When you introduce a new pattern, choose strongly contrasting groups of words and have small groups work under your direction. Students can practice the sort independently later in the week. As students deepen their understanding of a particular pattern, increase the challenge by using words with less contrast. Come back to sounds and patterns from time to time, contrasting them with new sounds and letters; don't teach a letter or a pattern for a week and then move on never to return.

For example, if I am teaching the hard /g/ sound and the letter *g* to beginning readers who are learning consonants, I am not going to contrast *g* words with *j* words—children just beginning to learn letter names will naturally confuse *g* and *j*. Instead I might begin by contrasting pictures of a *girl*, *gate*, *gas*, and *gorilla* with pictures of words

Figure 3–6 Word Sort

beginning with the /m/ sound—a clearer contrast and easier to learn. As students gain experience, I'll have kids sort *g* words within a grouping that also includes words beginning with several other letters they know. Eventually, they will compare words beginning with *g* with words beginning with *j* or compare words with *g* in the ending position with words having other letters in the ending position. Throughout I think through the appropriate generalizations aloud.

Various kinds of sorts—open, closed, speed, blind—require different levels of guidance. It's usually best to begin with more direction and provide less and less support as students deepen their understanding of a particular pattern or generalization. Rather than create your own word sorts, you can search for them online, but be a critical consumer: not everything you'll find will follow the principles recommended in this book. The sorts you find online need to meet the needs of *your* students in *your* groups as you have assessed them.

Open sorts. Begin teaching a new pattern with an open sort, in which students do not get any key words or headers directing them to sort in a particular way. Let students play with the words (or pictures) you choose for them and put them in groups based on whatever criteria they think are appropriate. This is a great formative assessment that reveals what students are noticing and thinking about. Allowed to sort the way he wants to, a student might sort by the number of letters in the word or some other less-than-optimal way. This tells me something about his problem-solving strategies and what he's paying attention to when looking at words. I then ask deliberate questions that get him thinking in new ways about the pictures and/or words in front of him: *What are you noticing? What other ways could you sort? Are you sorting by how the word looks or by the sounds you hear in that word or by the meaning?* A "gallery walk," in which students look at other students' sorts, also pushes their thinking. The following questions will prompt conversations about word learning:

- What did you learn from your sort?
- How might you apply what you learned to spell a new word with the same pattern?
- Why did you sort it this way?

Closed sorts. In a closed sort, you define the categories for students and give them a key word or picture (or both) for each column. Students learn faster when supported by teacher-directed sorts early in the year.

For example, if I want students to sort and compare words with the long-*a* and short-*a* sound, I might create an organizer that has a picture of a cat for short *a* and a picture of a cake for long *a*. I include a third column labeled *Oddballs*. I give students fifteen to twenty words like *cake, rain, man, map, chain,* and *bat,* perhaps including one or two words that don't have either *a* sound (*was* or *all,* for example). I model where a few words go by saying things such as "Hmmm. This word is *bat*. Let me stretch it out and see if the sound in the middle is more like *cake* or more like *cat*." After a few of these think-alouds, I let students sort the rest.

Have students practice completing additional sorts until they become fluent with the sounds or patterns they are studying. Always ask students to explain their sorts to you or to fellow students. Articulating the pattern and explaining their oddball exceptions to the pattern forces them to attend to similarities and differences.

Blind sorts. After students have repeated a number of closed sorts, introduce a blind sort (Bear et al. 2012), in which students hear the word spoken aloud rather than see it written down and write it in the correct category. Kids are usually quite successful with this activity and proud of what they have learned.

Here's an example. Still working on short and long *a*, I give students a sheet headed with the word and picture for *cat* (for short *a*), *cake* (for long *a*), and a column headed *Oddballs*. Earlier in the week,

I've led a sort in which they'd separated the words *make*, *page*, and *face* and from the words *mad*, *fast*, and *ask*. Today, instead of having them sort word cards, I dictate the words and ask the students to write them underneath the key word and/or picture representing the pattern the words contain. Afterward I show them the word cards so they can check their spelling. I include a few words we have *not* previously sorted—challenge words—to find out whether they are able to recognize the pattern in new words.

The oddballs keep kids thinking. If students know from the beginning that words can have short *a*, long *a*, or a different *a* sound altogether, they have to attend to the sounds carefully. And sometimes the exceptions lead students to notice a different pattern. For example, the oddballs *all*, *always*, and *although* (*a* combined with *l*) definitely do not contain the typical short- or long-*a* sound, but all three have the same beginning sound. Oddball words are a great way to introduce frequently encountered words like *have* or *said*. Imagine the sense of power students feel when they notice a pattern themselves and start to look for it in other words!

Speed sorts. After students have performed a sort under your direction and practiced it a few times, giving them speed sorts are fun and useful. Having students repeat a sort many times, trying to beat their best time, builds fluency and automaticity. Of course, it's not just about being fast. They also need to be accurate. I don't have students compare their time with their classmates' times. The point is setting a personal goal and beating it. Some students thrive trying to meet this type of goal, but you need to be cautious. Students who process information slowly can become frustrated, so you need to be observant. If you notice kids becoming frustrated or comparing their times to those of others, find other ways for them to repeat sorts until they achieve automaticity.

Choosing words. The spelling inventories I mention earlier in this section are a good starting point for deciding what words students should study. You can identify which patterns students have mastered and which ones they are ready to study by using an inventory, student writing samples, and running records. However, when choosing the actual words to use in sorts, there are a few more things to consider. As you introduce a new pattern, remember that a step backward is a step forward; that it is best to compare words that do with words that don't; and that over time you need to allow students to sort by sight, sound, and meaning.

Say I'm choosing words for a group of second graders I've assessed as being ready to begin studying long vowels. When students are first learning long vowels, I want them to understand how they are different from short-vowel sounds. I am most successful when I first ask students to sort pictures, so I give each child several pictures representing words that have a short-*a* sound and several that have a long-*a* sound. There might be pictures of a *cap*, a *map*, a *lap*, and a *tap* (representing short *a*) and a *cape*, an *ape*, *tape*, and *grapes* (representing long *a*). The students are thus able to compare the sound of long *a* to the sound of short *a*, which they already know. For this initial experience, I deliberately include only words ending in the /p/ sound, so the different vowel sound is more noticeable. As students put the pictures in groups and explain what is different, they compare the sounds of short-*a* words with long-*a* words and hear the difference. Although my target words are those containing the long-vowel sound, I include those with short-vowel sounds to help kids fully understand what is different. Knowing what a long-vowel sound is *not* is a great way to help them understand what it *is*.

Sorting by sight, sound, and meaning. Why do I start with pictures rather than words? Compare the printed words *cap, map, lap, tap* with *cape, ape, tape,* and *grape*. Obviously some have an *e* at the end and some don't: how much thinking would students have to do to sort them into two groups? While students need to know about the silent *e*, it is more important that they see the connection between the spelling pattern and the sound; therefore in the next sort, I include the words *and* the pictures.

When the kids are ready, I add the plural *s* and have kids sort *caps*, *maps*, *laps*, *taps*, *capes*, *apes*, *tapes*, and *grapes* along with the already familiar *cap*, *map*, *lap*, *tap*, *cape*, *ape*, *tape*, and *grape*. They see that the *s* ending changes the meaning a little—more than one—but also that the vowel sound does not change.

Now I can take one more step and have them compare the words *caps*, *maps*, *laps*, *taps*, *capes*, *apes*, *tapes*, and *grapes* with the words *bushes*, *lunches*, *dishes*, *taxes*, and *boxes* so they can discover patterns in the base word that affect the spelling. I set this up systematically. I have them sort the base words first, then place the plural forms underneath the singular ones. Then they highlight the base word and circle the part that means more than one. They pay attention to what happens when a word is pluralized because they take a step backward: they use words they already know and think about them in new ways. They can apply these generalizations later when spelling other words.

Word Study Notebooks

By keeping a word study notebook in which they record their thinking when they work with you in a small group and when they work independently, students create a trail of their word learning and their reflection on that learning. The notebook also contains poems that include the word patterns students are studying. Students read and reread these poems individually or with partners and highlight words with particular patterns; later they may read them aloud for the class. (More about using poems shortly.)

Games

Games are a great way to get students thinking about how words work. Students learning to spell ending consonant sounds could play dominos using blocks that have a letter on one side and a picture on the other, matching the picture with the letter they hear as the beginning (or ending) sound of the word the picture represents. Or long-vowel words can be entered on a blank game board; when students land on a space, they have to say another word with that same long-vowel sound (or pattern) to remain on the space.

A game students working on short vowels love is Show Me. Laminate construction paper, fold the bottom up to create a pocket, then fold in thirds, stapling the ends of the pocket down. Give students an assortment of letters used in the patterns they are working on, and have them take turns building words in their pocket. See Figure 3–7.

Word Lists and Charts

Anchor charts honor student thinking and help focus students' attention on the patterns they are studying. I begin by creating charts on which students can add their own examples of the word patterns we

Figure 3–7 Word Study Game

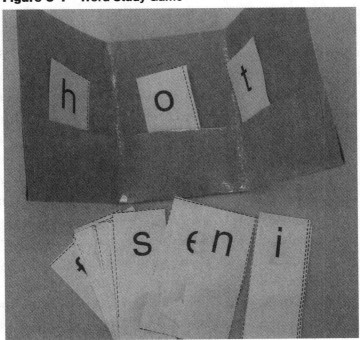

are studying, as well as oddballs. I'll start a chart when working on a sort with a small group, then encourage students to add words they discover in their reading. I set ground rules (for example, they can't add to the charts during a lesson), but having them add to the charts with bright-colored markers (what kid doesn't like to write with markers?) keeps them thinking about the word patterns. Because the words on the charts need to be spelled correctly, I stress accuracy and neat handwriting and give periodic reminders. I also provide "oops tape" (cut-up computer labels work well) so students can correct misspelled words. Students see that mistakes are part of the learning experience, not irreversible. When I run out of wall space, some of the charts go out into the hall, and other classes are challenged to add to them. Anchor charts build an atmosphere of shared inquiry around words and how they work; they allow students to build on one another's thinking.

Poetry

Comparing student's reading errors with their spelling inventories gives me a deeper understanding of how reading, writing, and spelling instruction are interconnected. I want my reading and spelling instruction to propel students' literacy synergistically. When students are ready to learn to spell a new pattern, I want them not only to sort and spell words that include those patterns but also to read texts containing those patterns, so they internalize the links. Poetry fills the bill.

The rhymes and alliteration in poetry offer numerous examples of the phonetic elements I want students to notice. A poem's brevity makes repeated readings nonthreatening, and rereading builds fluency. The vocabulary can be challenging, but when I choose poems carefully, students are excited about reading and rereading them and learn new vocabulary as well as the spelling patterns I want them to practice. Over the years I have collected—and organized by pattern—nursery rhymes, song lyrics, and limericks, along with the poems of Jack Prelutsky, Shel Silverstein, Brod Bagert, and many others. Remember this old nursery rhyme?

Do your ears hang low, do they wobble to and fro,

Can you tie 'em in a knot?

Can you tie 'em in a bow?

Can you throw 'em over your shoulder

Like a continental soldier?

Do your ears hang low?

I use this rhyme when I am working on the long-*o* sound. I compare the "ow" sound in *low* and *throw* with the short *o* in *wobble* and *knot* and discuss the *o* sound in *fro* and why that word and the word *to* have different sounds. I have to explain what a continental soldier is, but with a little support, almost every student can read this nursery rhyme and start thinking about how to spell the words in it.

I have my class read the same couple of poems every day for an entire week, always reading for meaning first and discussing the word choices the author made. The first day, I read the poems aloud as students listen; then we read them chorally a few times. On the second day we reread the poems, and I ask the kids to identify words that rhyme (or words that start with the same sound, or words that contain a particular pattern) and talk about what features are the same. I encourage students to be word detectives, paying attention to the aural, visual, and semantic patterns, as appropriate. On the third day we reread the poems again and review the patterns we observed the previous day. I hand out copies of the poems, and the students include them in their poetry notebook, reread them with a partner, and circle the words that include the pattern on which we are focusing. I also encourage students to notice words that fit the pattern in their independent reading and record these words on the back of the poem and on the classroom anchor charts. The last two days we reread the poems for fluency and review any new words entered on the anchor charts. Sometimes I add words from the poems to the sort we've been working on that week. If a poem lends itself to it, I have students think about how the alliteration or rhyming scheme affects the mood or meaning.

I often ask student pairs to reread poems from previous weeks so that they can review previous patterns and look for words that match the current pattern at the same time.

Word Walls

Students can better use word patterns to decode if the patterns are organized visually in some way. For example, you might create a word wall with five columns, one for each vowel—*a, e, i, o,* and *u.* Keep it simple, with few visual distractions, so that students can find individual words easily. Underneath each vowel, list key words from student sorts that contain rimes that include that vowel: words like *h<u>at</u>, h<u>ad</u>, m<u>ade</u>,* and *s<u>ay</u>* under *a* and words like *r<u>ed</u>, n<u>eed</u>, w<u>ent</u>,* and *<u>end</u>* under *e.* Separate short-vowel patterns, long-vowel patterns, and vowel digraphs within each column. I write the rime in red and the onset in black, to make it easy for students to find useful word parts (see Figure 3–8). You can also use another color to highlight digraphs or other word parts you want students to notice.

Talk with students about how they might compare and contrast these words. Use key words as a decoding strategy. For example, if a student gets stuck on the word *trade,* ask her to find a word on the wall that will help her: "What word in the *a* column looks most like *trade*?" (Point out *made* if she isn't sure.)

It's worthwhile to present minilessons about how students can use the word wall when reading on their own. Whenever a new key word or pattern is added, ask whether it's the same or different from other patterns already there. Connecting *-ade* to *-aid* and contrasting them both with *-ad* helps kids understand that some sounds can be spelled more than one way (often because of differences in meaning) and that long vowels are very different from short vowels. They learn that when they hear a long-*a* sound they may need to use other letters to mark the long-vowel pattern. Perhaps most important, they learn that the English language is more predictable than they thought.

Figure 3–8 Word Wall

Since I have different groups study different words, I color-code words by group, and students soon begin referring to and using words that other groups are working on. A word wall effectively supports students' ability to use analogy to decode.

Interactive Writing

A class journal is another essential tool for helping students internalize what they are learning about words. At the end of each day, we identify one important thing worth remembering and enter it in the journal using interactive writing (Craig 2006), so students can apply the skills they're learning in word study. They hold the marker and spell all the words they know, but I fill in the gaps, writing for them what they are not ready to write themselves and thinking aloud in order to provide the context they need to replicate this work on their own. (I include spelling generalizations based on my work with all the groups.)

For example, on a day when the students have attended an assembly program, we have a brief discussion about what we saw and learned.

Together we compose the following sentence: *We saw a man who played "Star Wars" on his trumpet.* Since they have already mastered the word *we*, I hand a student my marker, ask her where she would start writing, and let her write the word. I mention again that sentences start with a capital letter. Next I call on a student from the group that has been working on *aw*. He writes *saw* and explains how and why *saw* is spelled with an *aw*. I write any word or word part that is beyond my students' skills. Since the students have not studied *-ed* endings, I let a student write *play* and add the *-ed* ending while presenting a brief explanation.

Interactive writing lets students see why it's important to spell correctly. We share the class journal with visitors, and students take turns reading and rereading parts of it independently. They understand that we need to write legibly and that good spelling enables others to read and understand what we are trying to say. While I often do interactive writing with the whole class, it can also increase the intensity and focus of learning being undertaken by a group.

Independent Writing

Students need to write on their own every day. Writing should be taught daily and incorporated into all subject-area instruction wherever possible. (You might have your students keep math journals and science notebooks, for example.) At first their entries, especially those of younger students, may be mostly drawings, but as children grow in their ability to write and spell independently, the journals are great places in which to practice what students are learning about phonics. Writing gives word study purpose. Students understand why they need to learn how words work, that word study helps them communicate their ideas to others. Their writing is an important window into what they have learned, are learning, and are ready to learn next. (If you notice that several students are not consistently transferring what they know to their writing, you can work with them in a small group.)

The process of writing helps students think not only about phonetic patterns in words but about their meaning. Jonathan was a second grader who had been working on long-*a* patterns. He was trying to write the word *wait* in his science log. He first wrote: *Then you wat for the seed to gro*. He stared at the paper a while, looked up at the *cat* and *cake* anchor chart, erased *wat* and wrote *wate*. Even though that wasn't conventionally spelled, I was pleased. But Jonathan wasn't finished. He stared a while longer, then went over to the chart listing words that are pronounced the same but spelled differently. He looked at the words *weight* and *wait*, went back to his desk, erased *wate*, and wrote *wait*. I was thrilled! Jonathan hadn't asked me to help him spell; he problem-solved and came up with a conventional spelling!

Students need to be accountable for applying what they have learned. During word study you can ask them to look at what they are working on in writing workshop. Ask the students in a word-study small group to look at one another's writing and check the spelling of words that include the patterns they've been working on. Peer editing puts responsibility for applying learning in the hands of the students and helps connect word study with writing. Prompts that help students apply spelling generalizations include:

- What do you remember about long-*a* spelling patterns?
- Is there something in your word study notebook that will help you with that word?
- Listen to that vowel sound. What patterns do you know that might help you spell that word?
- Look at our word wall. Which of those words can help you spell that word?

Helping Kids Tackle More Complex Texts

Whether or not you are subject to the Common Core State Standards (CCSS), your students need to be able to handle increasingly challenging texts. The Common Core urges us to give students many opportunities to read nonfiction texts. Nonfiction often contains complex vocabulary, which certainly makes it more challenging. Word study, as outlined here, supports building students' ability to decode and figure out the meaning of new vocabulary.

For example, a colleague's students were reading a book about the civil rights movement and encountered the word *nonviolent*. That can be a tough word to decode, but the students had been working on short *e*. The word wall had *sent* on it, and there was an anchor chart containing words with the prefix *non-*, which students knew means *not*. These students had developed confidence from thoughtful word study and were interested in learning more about how words work. They didn't shy away from challenges like *nonviolent*; they looked at how the word was like other words they already knew. I was thrilled when one student realized how much the word *nonviolent* looked like *violet*, included on a chart of short-*e* words students found during word hunts.

Helping Students Notice and Name Letter, Sound, and Meaning Patterns

Teachers are hardwired to be helpful, and in the name of being helpful, we often cheat our students of opportunities to think. (I still struggle with this; I like being helpful and needed!) There is a fine line between being too helpful and not helpful enough, but we can better navigate it by being mindful of the words we use when we work with students. Small but deliberate changes in our teaching language can dramatically enhance student learning (see Figure 3–9).

Allowing Ourselves to Be Learners

I've come a long way in my thinking since facing that classroom of third graders struggling to spell words like *cumulus* on their spelling test. The classrooms I work in today are alive with groups of students who are thinking and problem-solving using words appropriate for their developmental level. There are no more worksheets, no more writing vocabulary words five times in order to memorize them. Students are applying their learning, not forgetting what they know about spelling when they write.

Figure 3–9 Language That Helps Students Develop Agency

Instead of telling a student she is wrong	ask her to explain her reasoning. Many times she will realize her error. Thank her for helping the class figure out something important. Miscues become an acceptable part of the thinking process, and you send a message that we learn from our mistakes. This encourages students to take risks and creates a learning-centered classroom.
Instead of answering students' questions	ask "What do you think?" before giving an answer. Turning responsibility over to students sets the expectation that they can figure it out themselves.
Instead of naming the rule or spelling generalization for students in teacher language	allow students to name the pattern or rule in kid language. This builds student ownership and is more likely to be remembered. Teacher language can come later.
Instead of telling students what they learned	allow students to tell what they learned and ask them to reflect on their learning process and how they problem-solved, thus teaching them to teach themselves. By internalizing a learning process themselves, they are not just learning a spelling pattern, they are learning how to learn.
Instead of focusing on right and wrong in student responses	focus on students' thinking. This helps students understand that their spelling ability can be improved with effort.

Once I saw that giving children opportunities to construct their own knowledge about how words work engaged them in ways my phonics worksheets never did, there was no turning back. Schools should be places in which we encourage thinking. The traditional methods for phonics and spelling I had been using didn't require a whole lot of thinking, just a whole lot of remembering—and my students were not always remembering, let alone applying!

The methods I was using to teach phonics and spelling did not require much thinking on my part either. I was teaching the way I had been taught. Asked whether teachers should encourage students to talk to one another, ask questions, think, and problem-solve as part of a learning community, I would have answered, "Yes, of course!" But the activities I assigned, which I assumed required students to think—word searches, writing words five times, worksheets—were only asking them to remember.

My learning journey has been gradual but constant, and my reflections about student learning (or lack of it), my professional reading, and the conversations I've had with my colleagues have driven the changes I've made. Looking back, the most important thing I've done has been to make the time to learn and grow. There are always pressing things to do—papers to grade, field-trip permission slips to send home, report card comments to write—but as a professional I have made time for my own personal learning.

We must be as thoughtful about our work as we want our students to be about theirs. We need to become our own researchers, fearlessly examining our students' reaction to our teaching. We need to open our classroom doors to colleagues who share our struggles and exchange ideas, learn, and grow together. We need to expand our conversations beyond the teacher next door and include our colleagues in the research community.

As my coauthor, Marcia, and I were writing this book, we found so much to talk about! Our dialogue, between researcher and classroom professional, has been rich and rewarding for both of us. This is no surprise; we are both teachers who want to improve student learning.

We encourage you to figure out how *you* learn best and incorporate learning into your day-to-day work. Will you visit other classrooms? Read professionally? Talk with others? Plan action research? Whatever method you choose, if you commit to it, your students will benefit. When you get stuck, do some research: you may find just the thing to jump-start your thinking in a new direction.

We need to be patient with ourselves and with our colleagues, understanding that real growth and change takes time. We need to allow time for new learning to take hold before we can tell whether it is working. We can't keep jumping to the next new thing, but we can't keep doing the same old thing if it's not working. As true professionals, we must be willing to make thoughtful changes when our students are not learning. We need to rely on and learn from one another over time. In this way we will deepen our own understanding of how words work and how to develop our students' understanding.

Marcia and I hope this book helps you on your own professional journey and that both you and your students stay engaged and thoughtful in your classroom.

AFTERWORD

ELLIN OLIVER KEENE

I hate to be the one to remind you, but can't you just see your six-year-old self drawing lines from the letter B to the picture of the bat? I was in Miss Gregg's first grade and I recall my frustration when I drew my shaky line to the wrong picture and tried to erase it. Paper tears were followed by big, salty tears (note the heteronym!).

Great news for kids—the joy is back in word study! As I read this book, I was reminded that word learning, when children work on spelling patterns at an appropriately challenging level, is more than a little fun and leads to leaps-and-bounds growth in independent reading and writing. I've observed many of the word-learning activities that Jennifer and Marcia describe and have literally heard peals of laughter and delight from young children. Just stand back and watch a group do a word sort and you'll see what I mean.

On a more serious note, I can't imagine, after reading this book, that anyone would continue to use one-size-fits-all phonics and spelling programs. Jennifer and Marcia have shown us that research does not support the skill-and-drill approach used in too many American classrooms to this day. They have acknowledged the complexity of word study, empathized with teachers who have struggled to move beyond worksheets, but have laid out an unambiguous route to much more effective word study methods. I am grateful on behalf of children who will have opportunities to learn the fundamentals of spelling and phonics in an authentic way, integrally tied to their daily reading and writing.

Jennifer Palmer and Marcia Invernizzi were the first two authors we asked to write for this series and we are proud of this important contribution to the field. I had read Jennifer's practical, wise responses to readers of *Mosaic of Thought* who shared their questions and ideas on the *Mosaic* listserv for years. Jennifer's guidance has always been practical, research-based, child-centered, and fun! I had, of course, read Marcia Invernizzi's work and have within arm's reach on my desk *Words Their Way*, now in its fifth edition. When Jennifer and Marcia signed on, Nell and I felt that we had found the dream team for this book and now you, no doubt, share our enthusiasm. Pass this book on to colleagues who you know will rediscover the fun in word study alongside their joyful young learners.

BIBLIOGRAPHY OF POETRY

This is by no means an exhaustive list. These books, some of which have been around a while and become children's classics, have been good sources of poetry to use to get students reading words with patterns that they are studying. I have also drawn on nursery rhymes and sometimes song lyrics as well.

Bagert, Brod. 1992. *Let Me Be the Boss: Poems for Kids to Perform.* Honesdale, PA: Boyds Mills Press.

Bagert, Brod. 1997. *The Gooch Machine: Poems for Children to Perform.* Honesdale, PA: Boyds Mills Press.

Dakos, Kali. 2003. *Put Your Eyes Up Here: And Other School Poems.* New York: Simon & Schuster.

Florian, Douglas. 1999. *Laugh-eteria.* Orlando, FL: Harcourt.

Hoberman, Mary Ann. 1991. *Fathers, Mothers, Sisters, Brothers.* New York: Scholastic.

Hudson, Wade, ed. 1993. *Pass It On: African-American Poetry for Children.* New York: Scholastic.

Katz, Alan. 2001. *Take Me Out of the Bathtub and Other Silly Dilly Songs.* New York: Simon & Schuster.

Katz, Bobbie. 1992. *Puddle Wonderful: Poems to Welcome Spring.* New York: Random House.

Lansky, Bruce, ed. 1994. *A Bad Case of the Giggles: Kids' Favorite Funny Poems.* Minnetonka, MN: Meadowbrook Press.

Lansky, Bruce, ed. 1999. *Miles of Smiles: Kids Pick the Funniest Poems, Book 3.* New York: Scholastic.

Lansky, Bruce, ed. 2000. *If Pigs Could Fly . . . and Other Deep Thoughts.* Minnetonka, MN: Meadowbrook Press.

Lansky, Bruce, ed. 2002. *My Dog Ate My Homework.* Minnetonka, MN: Meadowbrook Press. (Previously published with the title *Poetry Party.*)

Lenski, Loris. 1999. *Dirty Dog Boogie.* Toronto, ON: Annick Press.

Merriam, Eve. 1988. *You Be Good and I'll Be Night: Jump on the Bed Poems.* New York: William Morrow.

Nesbitt, Kenn. 2005. *When the Teacher Isn't Looking and Other Funny School Poems.* New York: Meadowbrook Press.

Prelutsky, Jack. 1982. *The Baby Uggs Are Hatching*. New York: Mulberry Books.

Prelutsky, Jack. 1984. *The New Kid on the Block*. New York: Scholastic.

Prelutsky, Jack. 1990. *Something Big Has Been Here*. New York: Greenwillow Books.

Prelutsky, Jack, ed. 1993. *A. Nonny Mouse Writes Again*. New York: Alfred A. Knopf.

Prelutsky, Jack. 1997. *It's Raining Pigs and Noodles*. New York: Greenwillow Books.

Shields, Carol Diggory. 2003. *Almost Late to School and Other School Poems*. New York: Puffin Books.

Silverstein, Shel. 1974. *Where the Sidewalk Ends*. New York: HarperCollins.

Silverstein, Shel. 1996. *Falling Up*. New York: HarperCollins.

REFERENCES

Aaron, P. G., S. Wilcznski, and V. Keetay. 1998. "The Anatomy of Word-Specific Memory." In *Reading and Spelling: Development and Disorders*, ed. C. Hulme and M. Joshi, 405–19. Mahwah, NJ: Lawrence Erlbaum Associates.

Abbott, T., and T. Jessell. 1999. *City in the Clouds*. Book 4 in The Secrets of Droon series. New York: Scholastic Paperbacks.

Arra, C. T., and P. G. Aaron. 2001. "Effects of Psycholinguistic Instruction on Spelling Performance." *Psychology in the Schools* 38 (4): 357–63.

Bandura, A. 1997. *Self-Efficacy: The Exercise of Control*. New York: Worth Publishers.

Barretta, G. 2010. *Dear Deer: A Book of Homophones*. New York: Square Fish.

Baumann, J. F. 2009. "Vocabulary and Reading Comprehension: The Nexus of Meaning." In The Handbook of Research on Reading Comprehension, 323–46. New York: Routledge.

Bear, D. R., K. Flanigan, L. Hayes, L. Helman, M. Invernizzi, F. J. Johnston, and S. Templeton. 2014. *Vocabulary Their Way: Words and Strategies for Academic Success*. Boston: Pearson Schools.

Bear, D. R., M. Invernizzi, S. Templeton, and F. Johnston. 2012. *Words Their Way: Word Study for Phonics, Vocabulary, and Spelling Instruction*. 5th ed. Boston: Pearson.

Bear, D. R., S. Negrete, and S. Cathey. 2012. "Developmental Literacy Instruction with Struggling Readers Across Three Stages." *New England Journal of Reading* 48 (1): 1–9.

Beers, J. W., and E. H. Henderson. 1977. "A Study of Developing Orthographic Concepts Among First Graders." *Research in the Teaching of English* 11 (2): 133–48.

Berninger, V., and M. Fayol. 2008. "Why Spelling Is Important and How to Teach It Effectively." In *Encyclopedia of Language and Literacy Development*, 1–13. London, ON: Canadian Language and Literacy Research Network. Available at www.literacyencyclopedia.ca/pdfs/topic.php?topId=234.

Berninger, V. W., K. Vaughan, R. D. Abbott, A. Brooks, K. Begayis, G. Curtin, and S. Graham. 2000. "Language-Based Spelling Instruction: Teaching Children to Make Multiple Connections Between Spoken and Written Words." *Learning Disability Quarterly* 23 (2): 117–35.

Block, M. K., and N. K. Duke. Forthcoming. "Letter Names Can Cause Confusion and Other Things Every Early Childhood Educator Should Know About English Orthography." *Young Children*.

Casar, M., R. Treiman, L. C. Moats, T. C. Polo, and B. Kessler. 2005. "How Do the Spellings of Children with Dyslexia Compare with Those of Nondyslexic Children?" *Reading and Writing: An Interdisciplinary Journal* 18: 27–49.

Cantrell, R. J. 2001. "Exploring the Relationship Between Dialect and Spelling for Specific Vocalic Features in Appalachian First-Grade Children." *Linguistics and Education* 12 (1): 1–23.

Cartwright, K. B., T. R. Marshall, K. L. Dandy, and M. C. Isaac. 2010. "The Development of Graphophonological-Semantic Cognitive Flexibility and Its Contribution to Reading Comprehension in Beginning Readers." *Journal of Cognition and Development* 11 (1): 61–85.

Chall, J. S. 1983. "Literacy: Trends and Explanations." *Educational Researcher* 12 (9): 3–8.

Chomsky, N., and M. Halle. 1968. *The Sound Pattern of English*. Cambridge, MA: MIT Press.

Clay, M. M. 1993. *An Observation Survey of Early Literacy Achievement*. Portsmouth, NH: Heinemann.

Craig, S. A. 2006. "The Effects of an Adapted Interactive Writing Intervention on Kindergarten Children's Phonological Awareness, Spelling, and Early Reading Development: A Contextualized Approach to Instruction." Journal of Educational Psychology 98 (4): 714–31. doi:10.1037/0022-0663.98.4.714

Dweck, C. S. 2007. "The Secret to Raising Smart Kids." *Scientific American Mind* 18 (6): 36–43.

Ehri, L. C. 1997. "Learning to Read and Learning to Spell Are One and the Same, Almost." In *Learning to Spell: Research, Theory, and Practice Across Languages*, ed. C. A. Perfetti, L. Reiben, and M. Fayol, 237–69. Mahwah, NJ: Lawrence Erlbaum Associates.

———. 2000. "Phases of Acquisition in Learning to Read Words and Implications for Teaching." *British Journal of Educational Psychology* (Monograph Series) 1: 7–28.

———. 2005. "Learning to Read Words: Theory, Findings, and Issues." *Scientific Studies of Reading* 9 (2): 167–88.

Flanigan, K. 2007. "A Concept of Word in Text: A Pivotal Event in Early Reading Acquisition." *Journal of Literacy Research* 39 (1): 37–70.

Flanigan, K., L. Hayes, D. Bear, S. Templeton, M. Invernizzi, and F. Johnston. 2011. *Words Their Way with Struggling Readers: Word Study for Reading, Vocabulary, and Spelling Instruction, Grades 4–12*. Boston: Pearson.

Ganske, K. 1999. "The Developmental Spelling Analysis: A Measure of Orthographic Knowledge." *Educational Assessment* 6: 41–70.

———. 2013. *Word Journeys: Assessment-Guided Phonics, Spelling, and Vocabulary Instruction*, 2d ed. New York: Guilford.

Gentry, J. R. 2007. *Assessing Early Literacy with Richard Gentry*. Portsmouth, NH: Heinemann.

Graham, S. 1999. "Handwriting and Spelling Instruction for Students with Learning Disabilities: A Review." *Learning Disability Quarterly* 22 (2): 78–98.

Gwynne, F. 1998a. *A Chocolate Moose for Dinner*. New York: Aladdin.

———. 1988b. *The King Who Rained*. New York: Aladdin.

Hanna, P. R., J. S. Hanna, R. E. Hodges, and H. Rudorf. 1966. *Phoneme–Grapheme Correspondences as Cues to Spelling Improvement*. Washington, DC: United States Office of Cooperative Research.

Helman, L. 2004. "Building on the Sound System of Spanish." *The Reading Teacher* 57: 452–60.

Henderson, E. H. 1990. *Teaching Spelling*. Boston: Houghton Mifflin.

Huang, F., and M. Invernizzi. 2012. "The Case for Confusability and Other Factors Associated with Lowercase Alphabet Recognition." *Applied Psycholinguistics* (December 7). doi:10.1017/S0142716412000604

Invernizzi, M., and L. Hayes. 2004. "Developmental Spelling Research: A Systematic Imperative." *Reading Research Quarterly* 39 (2): 216–28.

———. 2012. "Should the Focus of Literacy Education Be on 'Reading to Learn' or 'Learning to Read'?" Counterpoint. In *Debating Issues in American Education*, Vol. 2: *Curriculum and Instruction*, ed. A. J. Eakle, 82–89. New York: Sage.

Invernizzi, M., J. Meier, and C. Juel. 2003. Phonological Awareness Literacy Screening (PALS) 1–3. Charlottesville, VA: University Printing Services.

James, W. 1958. *Talks to Teachers on Psychology: And to Students on Some of Life's Ideals*. New York: W. W. Norton. Original work published in 1899 by Henry Holt & Co.

Johnston, F. R. 2000. "Word Learning in Predictable Text." *Journal of Educational Psychology* 92 (2): 248.

Johnston, P. H. 2004. *Choice Words: How Our Language Affects Children's Learning*. Portland, ME: Stenhouse.

Johnston, P. H., G. Ivey, and A. Faulkner. 2011. "Talking in Class: Remembering What Is Important About Classroom Talk." *The Reading Teacher* 65: 232–37.

Joshi, R. M., R. Treiman, S. Carreker, and L. C. Moats. 2008. "Isn't Spelling Just Memorizing Words? Answers to Some Common Questions About Spelling." *American Educator* 32 (4): 6–16.

Marciano, J. 2009. *Anonyponymous: The Forgotten People Behind Everyday Words*. New York: Bloomsbury.

Marshall, J. 1988. *Fox on the Job*. Illus. L. Barton. New York: Dial Books for Young Readers.

Morris, D., L. Blanton, W. E. Blanton, J. Nowacek, and J. Perney. 1995a. "Teaching Low Achieving Spellers at their 'Instructional Level.'" *Elementary School Journal* 92: 163–77.

Morris, D., L. Blanton, W. E. Blanton, and J. Perney. 1995b. "Spelling Assessment and Achievement in Six Elementary Classrooms." *The Elementary School* Journal 96: 145–62.

Morris, D., L. Nelson, and J. Perney. 1986. "Exploring the Concept of 'Spelling Instructional Level' Through the Analysis of Error-Types." *Elementary School Journal* 87: 181–200.

Nilsen, A. P., and D. L. F. Nilsen. 2004. *Vocabulary K–8: A Source-Based Approach*. Boston: Pearson.

Perfetti, C. A. 1997. "The Psycholinguistics of Spelling and Reading." In *Learning to Spell: Research, Theory, and Practice Across Languages*, ed. C. A. Perfetti, L. Rieben, and M. Fayol, 21–38. Mahwah, NJ: Lawrence Erlbaum Associates.

———. 2007. "Reading Ability: Lexical Quality to Comprehension." *Scientific Studies of Reading* 11 (4): 357–83.

Post, Y. V., and S. Carreker. 2002. "Orthographic Similarity and Phonological Transparency in Spelling." *Reading and Writing: An Interdisciplinary Journal* 15: 317–40.

Post, Y. V., S. Carreker, and G. Holland. 2001. "The Spelling of Final Letter Patterns: A Comparison of Instruction at the Level of the Phoneme and the Rime." *Annals of Dyslexia* 51 (1): 121–46.

Probst, J., and C. Tebbetts. 2013. *Stranded*. New York: Puffin.

Pullman, P. 2003. *The Golden Compass*. New York: Laurel Leaf.

Read, C. 1971. "Pre-school Children's Knowledge of English Phonology." *Harvard Educational Review* 41 (1): 1–34.

Rylant, C. 1990. *Henry and Mudge: The First Book*. New York: Aladdin.

Sameroff, A. J. 2009. "The Transactional Model." In *Transactional Model of Development: How Children and Contexts Shape Each Other*, ed. A. J. Sameroff, 3–21. Washington, DC: American Psychological Association.

Scanlon, D., and K. Anderson. 2011. *Early Intervention for Reading Difficulties: The Interactive Strategies Approach*. New York: Guilford.

Schlagal, R. 1989. "Constancy and Change in Spelling Development." *Reading Psychology* 10: 207–32.

———. 2002. "Classroom Spelling Inventories: History, Research, and Practice." *Reading Research and Instruction* 42: 44–57.

Templeton, S. 2007. "Instructional Approaches to Spelling: The Window on Students' Word Knowledge in Reading and Writing." In *Language and Literacy Learning in Schools*, ed. E. R. Silliman and L. C. Wilkinson, 273–91. New York: Guilford.

Templeton, S., D. R. Bear, M. Invernizzi, F. Johnston, K. Flanigan, D. R. Townsend, L. Helman, and L. Hayes. 2015. *Vocabulary Their Way: Word Study with Middle and Secondary Students*, 2d ed. New York: Pearson.

Terban, M. 1990. *Punching the Clock and Funny Action Idioms*. New York: Clarion.

———. 2007a. *In a Pickle*. New York: Clarion.

———. 2007b. *Mad as a Wet Hen*. New York: Clarion.

———. 2008. *Guppies in Tuxedos*. New York: Clarion.

Treiman, R. 1993. *Beginning to Spell*. New York: Oxford University Press.

Treiman, R., and D. C. Bourassa. 2000. "The Development of Spelling Skill." *Topics in Language Disorders* 20: 1–18.

Treiman, R., I. Levin, and B. Kessler. 2007. "Learning the Letter Names Follows Similar Principles Across Languages: Evidence from Hebrew." *Journal of Experimental Psychology* 96 (2): 87–106.

———. 2012. "Linking the Shapes of Alphabet Letters to Their Sounds: The Case of Hebrew." *Reading and Writing* 25 (2): 569–85.

Viise, N. n.d. "Feature Word Spelling Lists: A Diagnosis of Progressing Word Knowledge Through an Assessment of Spelling Errors." Unpublished Ph.D. diss., University of Virginia, 1994.

Vygotsky, L. 1978. *Mind in Society*. Cambridge, MA: Harvard University Press.

Worthy, M. J., and M. Invernizzi. 1989. "Spelling Errors of Normal and Disabled Students on Achievement Levels One Through Four: Instructional Implications." *Bulletin of the Orton Society* 40: 138–49.

Yolen, J. 1987. *Owl Moon*. New York: Philomel.